Treasures

A Reading/Language Arts Program

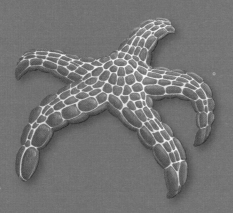

Mc Graw Hill **Macmillan McGraw-Hill**

Contributors

Time Magazine, Accelerated Reader

Students with print disabilities may be eligible to obtain an accessible, audio version of the pupil edition of this textbook. Please call Recording for the Blind & Dyslexic at 1-800-221-4792 for complete information.

A

The McGraw·Hill Companies

Mc Graw Hill **Macmillan McGraw-Hill**

Published by Macmillan/McGraw-Hill, of McGraw-Hill Education, a division of The McGraw-Hill Companies, Inc., Two Penn Plaza, New York, New York 10121.

Printed in the United States of America

ISBN-13: 978-0-02-198809-9/2, Bk. I
ISBN-10: 0-02-198809-9/2, Bk. I
4 5 6 7 8 9 (027/043) II 10 09 08

Treasures

Mc Graw Hill **Macmillan McGraw-Hill**

Unit 1

Relationships

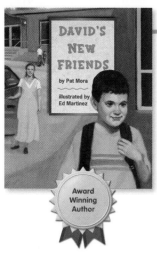

Award Winning Author

THEME: School Days

Award Winning Author

THEME: Making Friends

THEME: Firefighters at Work

Growth and Change

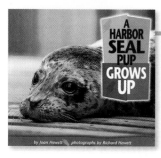

THEME: How Animals Grow

THEME: Staying Fit

Test Strategy: Author and Me

Unit 3

Better Together

Award Winning Author

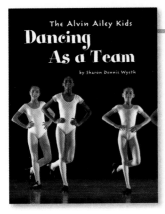

School
Days

Talk About It

What is it like to start a school year? What is the same and what is different from last year?

LOG ON Find out more about school days at **www.macmillanmh.com**

Vocabulary

tomorrow

groan

excited

whisper

carefully

different

Dictionary

When words are in alphabetical order, they are listed in ABC order.

The following words are in alphabetical order:

carefully
different
excited

School Is Starting!

by Josh Singh

Tom, Matt, and Lea played in the park. "Today is the last day of summer," said Tom. "**Tomorrow** is the first day of school!"

"The summer went by so fast," Matt said with a **groan**. He made a noise to show he was upset.

"We can't play all day when school starts," said Lea. "But I am still **excited**. I feel very happy about school this year. It's going to be fun!"

"I'm not so sure," Matt said.

"Really?" Lea asked Matt.

"I meant to **whisper** that," said Matt. "I wanted to say it softly. I did not want you to hear that I am scared."

Tom **carefully** climbed up the slide. He went up slowly so he would not fall. Then he slid down fast and smiled at Matt.

"It's okay, Matt," Tom said. "I am nervous, too. Second grade will be **different**. Nothing will be the same. But one thing is for sure. We will always be friends!"

Reread for **Comprehension**

Story Structure
Character and Setting

Thinking about a story's structure, or the way it is organized, can help you understand more about the characters and the setting. Reread the story and use the chart to help you understand the people in the story and where it takes place.

Character	Setting

Comprehension

Genre
Realistic Fiction is a made-up story that could happen in real life.

Story Structure
Character and Setting
As you read, use your Character and Setting Chart.

Character	Setting

Read to Find Out
What is David like? Think about what he says and does in the story.

DAVID'S NEW FRIENDS

by Pat Mora

illustrated by
Ed Martinez

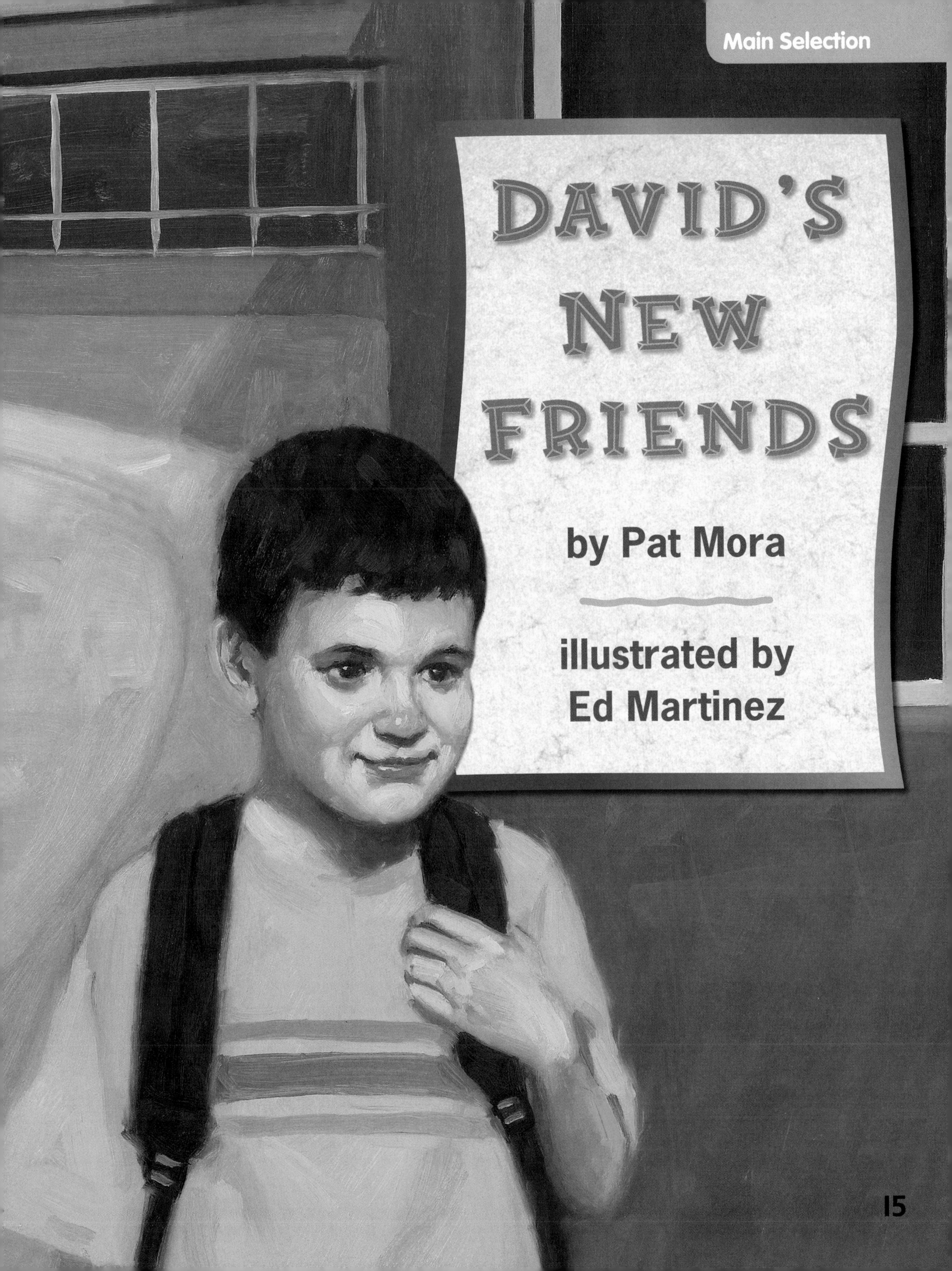

"**Tomorrow** is the first day of school, David,"
Mom says. "Are you glad?"

"I guess."

My mom is a teacher. She really likes school.
I like school, too, but the first day is **different**.
Everything is new.

My sister Linda asks me to read to her. She hands me a book about lizards.

"Ugh," I **groan**. "Let's read about tigers. I don't like creepy lizards."

I read to my sister, but I think about school, too. Will I like my teacher? Will I meet new friends?

The next morning, Grandma hands me my backpack. "You are a big boy now," she says. "You're in second grade!"

I try to act big. Then I give her a hug.

Mom drives me to school.

"Aren't you **excited**, David? You're going to see your school friends."

"Yes," I answer. But also I hope I'll meet some new ones, too.

My new classroom is full of neat stuff. Maybe this year *will* be fun.

I see Ron and Josie near the fish tank. I want to tell them about my trip to the zoo. Then I see the lizard. Ugh! I sit on the other side of the room.

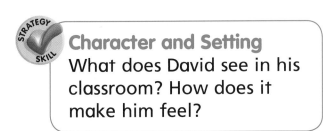

STRATEGY SKILL

Character and Setting
What does David see in his classroom? How does it make him feel?

Our teacher is standing by the chalkboard.
"Good morning, girls and boys," he says. "I'm your
new teacher, Mr. Roy." He gives the class a big grin.
Then he looks around. "Where's the chalk?"
he asks.

I get up and hand him some chalk.

Mr. Roy smiles. "Thanks, David."

"Okay," Mr. Roy says. "Let's begin!" He looks around. "Now, where are my glasses?"

I point to his head.

"What are you doing up there?" he asks his glasses. Everyone laughs. Mr. Roy gives me a wink.

I like this teacher.

We finish math at 10:00. Then it's snack time. Everyone gets juice to drink. Mr. Roy spills some on his shoes. I give him my napkin.

Mr. Roy says to me, "Oh no, David! These are my slippers. I was so excited this morning, I forgot to put on my shoes!" We laugh together.

"Okay, girls and boys," says Mr. Roy. "It's time to meet a friend of mine." He picks up the lizard.

"Oh no!" I say to myself. "Not the lizard!"

"His name is Slim," says Mr. Roy. "He's thin like me."

The class giggles.

Mr. Roy says, "I hold him **carefully** so I don't hurt him."

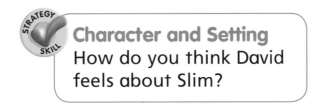

Character and Setting
How do you think David feels about Slim?

23

Just then, Slim slips out of Mr. Roy's hand.
Everyone starts yelling.
Slim is as fast as a whip.

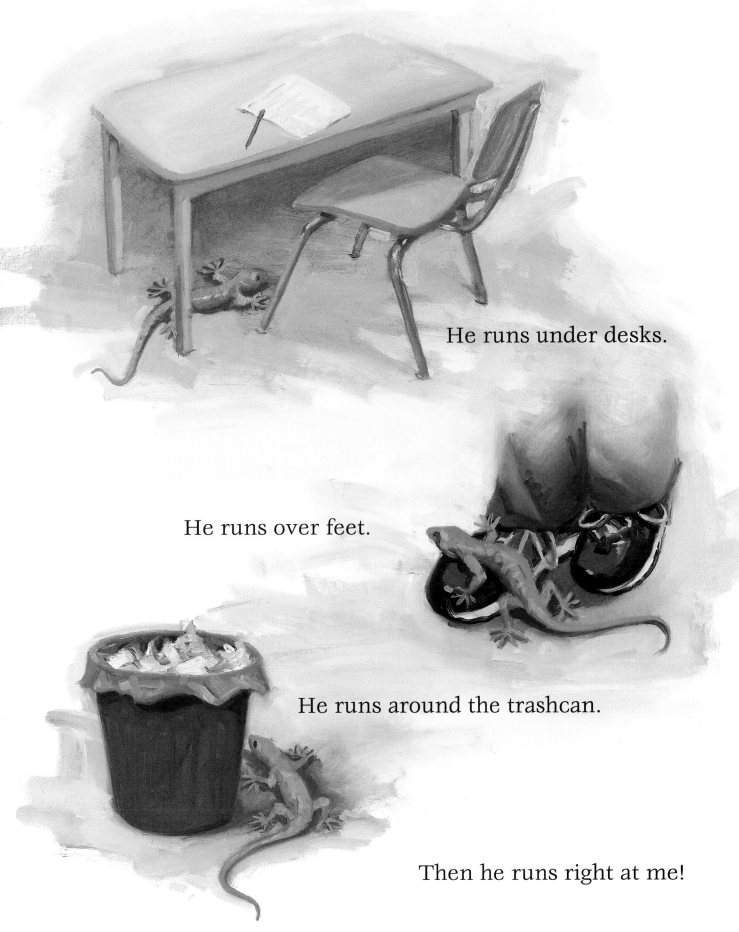

He runs under desks.

He runs over feet.

He runs around the trashcan.

Then he runs right at me!

"Catch him, David!" yells Mr. Roy.

I take a deep breath and drop to my knees.

All the kids stay very still. Everyone is watching me.

"Here, Slim," I **whisper**. "I won't hurt you."
I move very slowly. I get closer and closer.
I look into Slim's bright eyes, and then—
I GRAB HIM!

I feel Slim wiggle in my hands. I can tell that he's afraid.

"Don't worry, Slim," I say quietly. "We won't hurt you."

I put Slim back in the tank. He runs under a twig and then peeks out. He winks at me!

Mr. Roy says, "I think he likes you, David."

I think I like him, too.

At the end of the day, Mr. Roy stops me at the door. "Thanks for your help today, my friend," he says smiling.

Grandma and Linda are waiting for me after school.

"Wow!" I say. "I have a great new teacher. He's my friend. And guess what?"

"What?" asks Linda.

"I have another friend, too. His name is Slim. He's a lizard!"

MEET NEW FRIENDS PAT AND ED

Author **PAT MORA** says many of the ideas for her books come from the things she likes best. Some things she likes are families and folk tales. Pat is special because she can speak and write in both English and Spanish!

When artist **ED MARTINEZ** was in college, he saw a TV show about children's book illustrators. He decided then that he wanted to illustrate books too.

Other books written by Pat Mora

Find out more about Pat Mora and Ed Martinez at **www.macmillanmh.com**

Author's Purpose
Pat Mora wrote this story for you to enjoy. Think about your first day of second grade. Who did you meet? Write about that day.

Comprehension Check

Retell the Story

Use the Retelling Cards to retell the story.

Retelling Cards

Think and Compare

1. How does David feel about school when he is at home? Does he feel **different** after the first day?
   Story Structure: Character and Setting

Character	Setting

2. Reread pages 16–19. How does David feel before he goes to school? Use the text to explain how you know. **Analyze**

3. Would you like to have Mr. Roy as your teacher? Why or why not? **Evaluate**

4. Why might David think lizards are creepy? **Analyze**

5. Read "School Is Starting" on pages 12–13. How is Matt like David? Tell how you know.
   Reading/Writing Across Texts

Who's Who at School?

by Gail Riley

Welcome back to school! Many people work together to help you work, learn, and play. Do you know who is who?

As the leader of the school, I have an office in the school building. I hire the teachers. I make the school rules and help everyone follow them. Who am I? I am the **principal**.

The principal is the leader of the school.

The librarian helps you find books.

I take care of the books and other materials in the school library. If you need to find a good book to read, I can help you choose one. Sometimes I also read out loud to you. Who am I?

I am the **librarian**.

When you are sick at school, I will help you. You can come to my office to lie down until you feel better. I also teach you how to stay healthy. Who am I? I am the **nurse**.

We make meals in your school's kitchen. Early in the morning we start to make your breakfast and lunch. Sometimes we help clean the tables where you eat. Who are we? We are lunchroom workers.

My job is creating a place for you to learn. I plan your lessons for each day. I also answer your questions and correct your homework. Who am I?

I am a teacher.

A teacher helps you learn.

All of these people do important work in your school. Someone else does important work, too. Who is it?

You!

Connect and Compare

1. How do the captions and photos give you more information about who's at school? **Photos and Captions**

2. Think about the story *David's New Friends*. If David wanted to learn more about lizards, which school worker would he see? Why? **Reading/Writing Across Texts**

  Social Studies Activity

Interview a school worker to find out what he or she does. Write a description of the person's job.

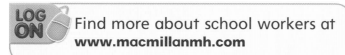 **LOG ON** Find more about school workers at **www.macmillanmh.com**

35

Writer's Craft

Topic Sentence
Good writers use a strong topic sentence at the beginning of a paragraph.

My topic sentence tells the main idea of the paragraph.

I asked a question and ended it with a question mark.

Ready for School!

by Eileen S.

Today was the first day of school. I was so excited I woke up very early. I decided to wear my red pants and my lucky striped socks. Then I sat down to eat breakfast.

The next thing I knew, my mom was shaking me. I had wet hair. My face was sticky. What happened? I had fallen asleep in my cereal bowl!

Your Turn

Think about your first day of school. What did you do that day? How did you feel? Write about it. Use a strong topic sentence to grab the reader's attention. Use the Writer's Checklist to check your writing.

Writer's Checklist

☐ **Ideas:** Did I use a strong topic sentence to grab the reader's attention?

✓ **Voice:** Did I tell how I felt about the day?

✓ **Conventions:** Did I end each statement with a period? Did I end each question with a question mark?

✓ **Sentence Fluency:** Did I vary how I began my sentences?

Making Friends

Talk About It

What does being a friend mean to you?

 Find out more about making friends at **www.macmillanmh.com**

Making Muffins and a Friend

by Vanessa Lavin

"Don't forget," Ms. Kim said. "Tomorrow you must bring in something to **share** with the class. Please bring something that all of us can look at. It could be a book that you **enjoyed**. You can tell us why you liked it so much."

Pam's friends had **wonderful** ideas. Pam did not have any great ideas like theirs. After the bell rang, the class began **thinning** out. The students left the classroom one by one. Soon only Pam and Marco were left. Pam asked Marco about his idea.

"I think I might cook," he said. "Let's make something together!"

They decided to make muffins. Pam was **delighted**. She was very happy to have an idea at last.

Making muffins was not easy. The mix was too thick. They had to add a lot of milk to fix it. The muffins were not perfect, but Pam and Marco did not care. Being together was fun. The best thing to share was the **company** of a new friend!

Reread for **Comprehension**

Story Structure
Plot
Thinking about a story's structure, or the way it is organized, can help you understand the plot. The plot is what happens at the beginning, middle, and end of the story. Reread the story and use the chart to describe the plot.

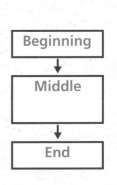

Beginning
↓
Middle
↓
End

Comprehension

Genre
Fiction is a story with made-up characters and events.

Story Structure
Plot
As you read, use your Story Map.

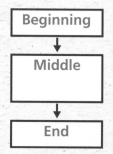

Beginning

↓

Middle

↓

End

Read to Find Out
What happens to Mr. Putter in the beginning, middle, and end of this story?

42

Mr. Putter & Tabby Pour the Tea

by Cynthia Rylant
illustrated by Arthur Howard

Award Winning Author

44

1

Mr. Putter

Before he got his fine cat, Tabby,
Mr. Putter lived all alone.

In the mornings he had no one
to **share** his English muffins.
In the afternoons he had no one
to share his tea.

And in the evenings
there was no one
Mr. Putter could
tell his stories to.
And he had the
most **wonderful**
stories to tell.

All day long as Mr. Putter
clipped his roses
and fed his tulips
and watered his trees,
Mr. Putter wished for
some **company**.

He had warm muffins to eat.

He had good tea to pour.

And he had wonderful stories to tell.

Mr. Putter was tired of living alone.

Mr. Putter wanted a cat.

Plot

Why does Mr. Putter want a cat at the beginning of the story?

Tabby

Mr. Putter went to the pet store.

"Do you have any cats?" he asked the
pet store lady.

"We have fourteen," she said.

Mr. Putter was **delighted**.

But when he looked into the cage,
he was not.

"These are kittens," he said.
"I was hoping for a cat."
"Oh, no one wants cats, sir,"
said the pet store lady.
"They are not cute.
They are not peppy."

Mr. Putter himself had not
been cute and peppy for a
very long time.
He said, "I want a cat."
"Then go to the shelter, sir,"
said the pet store lady.
"You are sure to find a cat."

Mr. Putter went to the shelter.
"Have you any cats?"
he asked the shelter man.
"We have a fat gray one,
a thin black one,
and an old yellow one," said the man.
"Did you say old?" asked Mr. Putter.

The shelter man brought Mr. Putter
the old yellow cat.
Its bones creaked,
its fur was **thinning**,
and it seemed a little deaf.
Mr. Putter creaked,
his hair was thinning,
and he was a little deaf, too.

So he took the old yellow cat home.

He named her Tabby.

And that is how their life began.

Mr. Putter and Tabby

In the mornings
Mr. Putter and Tabby liked to share
an English muffin.
Mr. Putter ate his with jam.
Tabby ate hers with cream cheese.

In the afternoons
Mr. Putter and Tabby
liked to share tea.
Mr. Putter took his with sugar.
Tabby took hers with cream.

And in the evenings
they sat by the window,
and Mr. Putter told stories.
He told the most wonderful stories.
Each story made Tabby purr.

On summer days they warmed their
old bones together in the sun.
On fall days they took
long walks through the trees.
And on winter days they turned
the opera up *very* loud.

Mr. Putter could not remember
life without Tabby.
Tabby could not remember
life without Mr. Putter.
They lived among their
tulips and trees.

60

They ate their muffins.

They poured their tea.

They turned up the opera,
and **enjoyed** the most
perfect company of all—
each other.

STRATEGY SKILL

Plot
What does Mr. Putter do in
each chapter of this story?

63

Cat "Mews" From Cynthia and Arthur

Cynthia Rylant has written many books. When she gets an idea, she says, "I sit down with pen and paper, and soon I've got a story going!" She has two cats named Boris and Blossom. Boris gets into trouble, but "Blossom is perfect," Cynthia says. Which cat do you think is like Tabby?

Arthur Howard illustrates all of the Mr. Putter and Tabby books. When Arthur started the series, he drew Mr. Putter to look like his father. He based Tabby on his mother's cat, Red.

 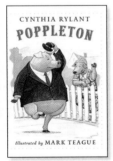

Other books written by Cynthia Rylant

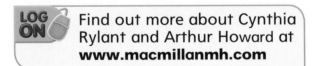
LOG ON Find out more about Cynthia Rylant and Arthur Howard at **www.macmillanmh.com**

Author's Purpose

Cynthia Rylant wrote this story about a man and his special cat to make you smile. Write about a person or an animal you know.

64

Comprehension Check

Retell the Story

Use the Retelling Cards to retell the story.

Retelling Cards

Think and Compare

STRATEGY SKILL

1. Why does Mr. Putter want **company**? How does this change by the end of the story?
Story Structure: Plot

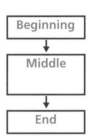

```
Beginning
   ↓
Middle

   ↓
End
```

2. Reread pages 54–55. Why does Mr. Putter pick Tabby over another cat? Use the text to explain why. **Evaluate**

3. Would you like having Tabby for a pet? Why or why not? **Synthesize**

4. Why do you think the pet store lady tells Mr. Putter to go to the shelter to look for a cat? Explain. **Synthesize**

5. Read "Making Muffins and a Friend" on pages 40–41. How are Pam and Marco like Mr. Putter and Tabby? **Reading/Writing Across Texts**

Social Studies

Genre

An Essay is written to persuade a reader about something.

SKILL

Text Feature

A List shows a series of items in a certain order.

Content Vocabulary

trust

friendship

promise

Rules of Friendship

by Abigail Jones

A friend is someone you know and **trust**. Friends do things together. They listen to each other and share their feelings.

Everything is better when you have a friend to share it with! This is why **friendship** is important.

Friendship Rules

1. Share. It's important to take turns.
2. Be kind.
3. Tell the truth.
4. Be a good listener.
5. Keep your **promises**. Remember to do what you say you will.
6. Help each other.
7. Always make room for a new friend!

When you follow this list of rules you may keep friendships for a long time. Following these rules can also help you make new friends. Try to make a new friend today!

Connect and Compare

1. How does the list of rules help you understand what friendship is? **List**

2. Think about the rules of friendship and *Mr. Putter and Tabby Pour the Tea.* Which rules do Mr. Putter and Tabby follow? How can you tell? **Reading/Writing Across Texts**

 Social Studies Activity

Research what it means to be a good friend. Ask others what they think makes someone a good friend. Then write your own list of rules.

LOG ON Find more about friendship at **www.macmillanmh.com**

Write About a Friend

I wrote a topic sentence that tells the main idea.

This detail, an exclamation, tells why I feel strongly about my friend.

My Funny Friend
by Benny B.

My best friend Jenny lives next door to me. We have been friends since we were four years old. Jenny has freckles and long, red hair. She also wears glasses just like I do! Jenny likes to tell jokes and riddles. When I want to laugh, I go visit my favorite funny friend!

Your Turn

Write about a friend or someone you know well. Tell what the person is like. Tell about how the person looks or sounds. Tell what you like to do together. Use the Writer's Checklist to check your writing.

Writer's Checklist

☐ **Ideas:** Did I write a good paragraph with a topic sentence and supporting details?

☑ **Word Choice:** Did I use words that give strong details that tell about the person?

☑ **Conventions:** Does each sentence end with the correct end mark? Did I end exclamations with exclamation marks?

☑ **Organization:** Did I include a good ending for my narrative?

Talk About It

How do firefighters help people?

 Find out more about firefighters at **www.macmillanmh.com**

Firefighters at Work

Vocabulary

safe

flames

tell

forest

heat

A firefighter from Engine Company 16 jumps rope with neighborhood kids.

Firehouse Friendships

A firehouse is a place where firefighters come to work. They keep neighborhoods **safe** by fighting fires. They help save people from the smoke and **flames** of a fire.

At Engine Company 16 in Chicago, firefighters help in other ways. They welcome neighborhood children inside the firehouse. The firefighters show children what to do in case of a fire. The firefighters and the children become good friends.

72

A Special Bear

Smokey Bear is a made-up character. Rangers use Smokey to **tell** about the danger of **forest** fires. They want people to be safe in the woods. Smokey says, "Only YOU can prevent forest fires."

Smokey tells people to be careful in the woods. He says to tell a ranger if you smell smoke or see fire. Get away from the fire quickly. Heavy smoke can make it hard to breathe.

Forest fires give off so much **heat** that plants can die. It is too hot for them to grow anymore.

Smokey says, "Only YOU can prevent forest fires."

SMOKEY SAYS—
Care <u>will</u> prevent 9 out of 10 forest fires!

This is what Smokey looked like in 1945.

LOG ON
Find out more about fire safety workers at **www.macmillanmh.com**

Fighting the Fire

What happens when a fire breaks out in a forest?

One day the sky over the **forest** in LaVerne, California, filled with smoke. The people who lived nearby knew what it meant. They knew a fire was close. The smoke made it hard to see and to breathe. People were afraid they would choke.

Firefighters face a wall of fire
in California in 2003.

A wildfire can do a lot of damage to a
forest. It can kill trees and animals. The
people who lived near the forest did not feel
safe. They hoped that the firefighters would
arrive soon.

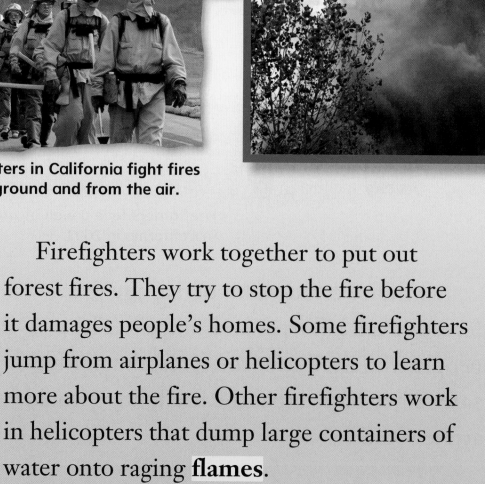

Firefighters in California fight fires on the ground and from the air.

Firefighters work together to put out forest fires. They try to stop the fire before it damages people's homes. Some firefighters jump from airplanes or helicopters to learn more about the fire. Other firefighters work in helicopters that dump large containers of water onto raging **flames**.

Firefighters help people, too. They **tell** them to get away from the fire. They save people who might be trapped. Firefighters use special clothing to protect their bodies from the **heat**. Firefighters work very hard until the fire is out. They know that people's lives and homes depend on them.

A family watches as flames come near their neighborhood.

Think and Compare

STRATEGY SKILL

1. What is the main idea of this article?

2. Why are wildfires harmful?

3. Why are firefighters important people in your neighborhood?

4. After reading this article and "A Special Bear," do you think Smokey can help prevent forest fires? Why or why not?

Different Ways to Put Out a Fire

Firefighters put out all kinds of fires. In the city, they use fire trucks with long ladders. These ladders help reach people inside tall buildings. They also help firefighters get their hoses closer to the fire.

Wildfires strike on mountains and in forests. It is hard to reach these places. Firefighters use helicopters to fly above the fire. They drop water or chemicals onto the fire to help put it out.

Sometimes fires can start in boats on the water. Firefighters use fireboats to put out this kind of fire. These boats have pumps that use water from the river, lake, or ocean to help put out the fire.

Fire Equipment Chart

Location of Fire	Equipment Used
City	fire trucks with ladders
Forest	airplanes and helicopters
Water	fireboats with pumps

Go On ▶

Directions: Answer the questions.

1. Firefighters use ladders to

   A fight wildfires.

   B climb mountains.

   C reach people inside tall buildings.

   D drop water.

2. Why are helicopters used to fight wildfires?

   A They can fly above a fire.

   B They can pump water.

   C They bring hoses closer to fires.

   D They have ladders.

3. Suppose a fire starts in a boat on the water.
   Which equipment would be used?

   A a fire truck

   B a helicopter

   C a ladder

   D a fireboat

4. How is putting out a wildfire different from
   putting out a fire in a tall building?

5. Summarize the article. Use the chart on
   page 78 to help you write your summary.

STOP 79

Write to a Prompt

Write a story about a time when
you helped out.

My story has a
lot of details.

Mrs. Clay and the Snowy Day

    Mrs. Clay is our neighbor and our
friend. She cannot do all the things she
used to do. Last winter there was a big
snowstorm. The street and the grass
all turned white.

    My big brother and I wanted to help
Mrs. Clay. We asked her if we could shovel
her driveway. It was hard work! When we
were finished, Mrs. Clay invited us inside
her house for some hot chocolate. We were
glad we had helped our friend.

Your Writing Prompt

Have you ever helped anyone? What did you do? How did it make you feel? Write a story about a time you helped someone. Use details to tell your story.

Writer's Checklist

- ☑ Think about your purpose for writing.

- ☑ Plan your writing before beginning.

- ☑ Be sure your story has details.

- ☑ Use your best spelling, grammar, and punctuation.

Talk About It

Every person is
different. What
makes you special?

LOG ON Find out more about
being yourself at
www.macmillanmh.com

Being Yourself

Vocabulary

cultures

deaf

language

signing

relatives

celebrate

Dictionary

You can use a dictionary or other reference books to look up **new meanings for words you know**.

signing: showing words and letters with your hands and fingers. *verb*.

A Special Camp

by Kate Jones

Camp Taloali (ta-loe-AL-ee) in Oregon is a special place. The campers and counselors come from many backgrounds and **cultures**. Almost everyone at Taloali is **deaf**, which means they cannot hear.

If campers cannot hear, how do they know what someone is saying to them? One way is through sign **language**. Sign language is a way that people can talk to one another without speaking. **Signing** is a way to show words and letters with your hands and fingers. It's like a code.

Some **relatives** of deaf children started Camp Taloali. They wanted the deaf people in their family to have a camp like hearing children have.

At the end of each summer, the campers **celebrate** with a big party. They remember all the fun times they had together. Then they sign good-bye to their new friends.

Reread for **Comprehension**

Summarize
Main Idea and Details
One way to summarize is to state the main idea, or the most important idea in an article. Details give more information about the main idea. Reread the article and use the chart to help you understand the main idea and details.

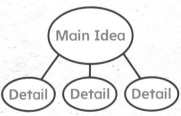

Comprehension

Genre
A **Photo Essay** uses mostly photographs to give information about a topic.

Summarize
Main Idea and Details
As you read, use your Main Idea and Details Web.

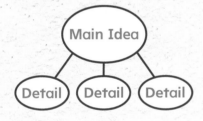

Read to Find Out
Who is Rosina? Tell what you find out about her.

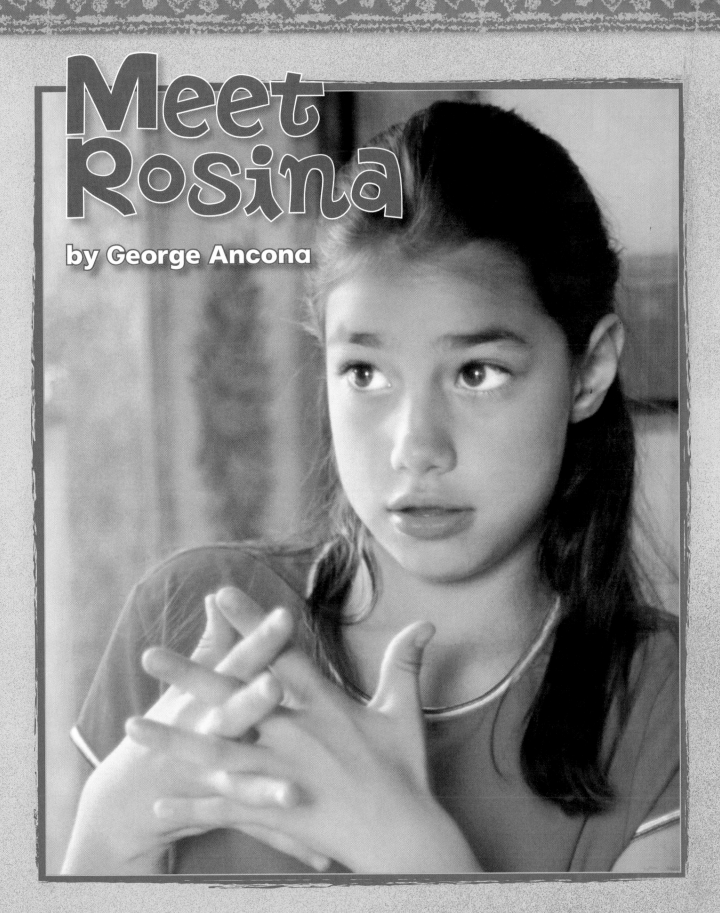

Meet Rosina

by George Ancona

Hi!   I'm

R o s i n a

I am **deaf**, so I talk with my hands.

I go to the New Mexico School for the Deaf. All of our teachers teach with American Sign **Language**. We call this **signing**.

We study math, writing, reading, and art. We also play sports. It's the same as in other schools.

Main Idea and Details
How would you describe Rosina's school?

My brother Emilio also goes to my school. After lunch, we play basketball during recess.

My mom and aunt are deaf, too. They work at the school. Mom is a teacher's helper.

Mom came from Mexico when she was little. She had to learn American Sign Language so that she could learn English. That's because each country has its own way of signing.

Aunt Carla's job is to help students and teachers learn about different **cultures**. She also takes care of the school museum.

In the museum there are pictures of our **relatives** who went to the school. Aunt Carla often tells me fun stories about when my parents were younger. She told me that my parents met each other at a high school dance.

Sometimes we go to the school library.
Our librarian, Hedy, signs stories from the
books in the library.

Hedy is very good at telling stories. She makes us feel as if we're in the story. The story can make us feel sad, scared, worried, or happy.

95

I love going to art class. I like to paint using watercolors. Here I am painting a picture of myself!

Too Many Hands??

Story and Art by
The Children of the
Second Grade,
**New Mexico School
for the Deaf**

When we were in second grade, our class made up a story. It was about a deaf dad who woke up one day with four arms. We wrote it and did all the drawings. Then we made it into a book called *Too Many Hands*.

Our book was published! Today we had a book signing. We wrote our names in the books that people bought.

I like sports. This year I am playing rugby. The way we play is to tag the person carrying the ball. Then he or she throws it to another player on the team. By running fast we can get away and cross the goal line.

Our team played other schools at the end of the year. We beat all the other teams and won a big trophy.

Then we wanted to **celebrate**. We splashed our coach with cold water. Some of us got wet, too. We were just joking, so no one got mad.

After school I shower and change clothes for dinner. Mom likes to fix my hair. She puts it up in a bun like her mother did.

At home we all help Mom cook Mexican meals. While I chop the lettuce, Emilio cuts up cheese. Dad makes the guacamole. Then I fry the tacos.

After dinner, Dad and I play a game of chess. Emilio roots for me. He's hoping that I win, but Dad wins anyway.

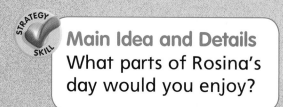

Main Idea and Details
What parts of Rosina's day would you enjoy?

Mom, Dad, Emilio, and me. That's my family—but there are many more, too.

We are a big family. I have lots of uncles, aunts, cousins, grandpas, and grandmas. My father's family was among the first Spanish people that came to New Mexico. That was 500 years ago.

Most of my mom's family is deaf. My whole family uses sign language to talk to each other.

This is how we sign "goodbye."

Taking Photos and Making Smiles with George Ancona

George Ancona wrote the words and took the photographs for this selection. He learned how to take photographs from his father when he was growing up. His father developed pictures in their bathroom!

Today, George likes to photograph people in their everyday lives. Meeting all kinds of people is what he enjoys the most. Before George wrote this book, he already knew some sign language. In this picture, he is signing, "I love you!"

Other books written by George Ancona

 Find out more about George Ancona at **www.macmillanmh.com**

Author's Purpose

George Ancona wanted to tell us about Rosina's day. Write a journal entry about what you did yesterday.

Comprehension Check

Retelling Cards

Retell the Story

Use the Retelling Cards to retell the selection.

Think and Compare

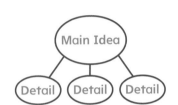

1. How does Rosina spend most of her day? What are her favorite activities? **Summarize: Main Idea and Details**

2. Reread page 97. How does Rosina feel about the book that she and her class wrote? Use the text to explain. **Analyze**

3. How is your day like Rosina's day? How is it different? **Analyze**

4. Rosina's family is also **deaf**. How does this help or not help Rosina? Explain. **Apply**

5. Read "A Special Camp" on pages 84–85. Do you think Rosina would like to go to Camp Taloali? Explain. **Reading/Writing Across Texts**

YOU-TÚ

by Charlotte Pomerantz

WHO ARE YOU?

You are you.	Tú eres tú.
Not me,	No yo,
But you.	Pero tú.
Look in the mirror	Mira al espejo
Peek-a-boo	Peek-a-boo
The face that you see	La cara que miras
Isn't me—	No soy yo—
It's you.	Eres tú.

Connect and Compare

1. Where are the rhyming words in this poem? **Rhyme**

2. Think about the poem and *Meet Rosina.* How do you think Rosina would feel about this poem? Explain why.
Reading/Writing Across Texts

 Find out more about rhyming poems at **www.macmillanmh.com**

Write an E-mail

I wanted to tell important details about me. Here is what I wrote.

Each detail sentence has a predicate and tells a complete thought.

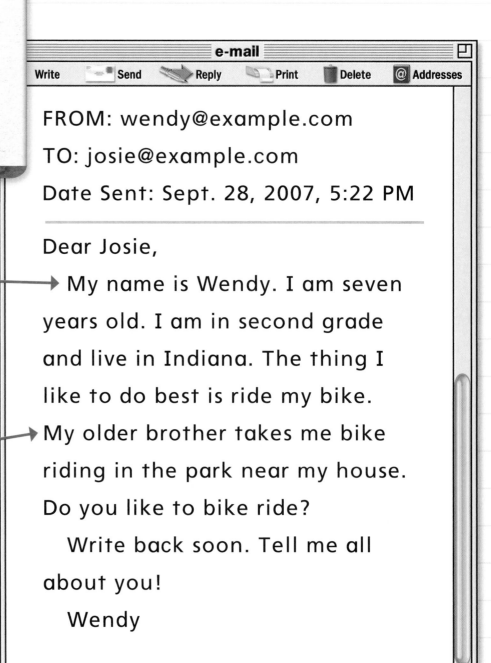

e-mail

Write Send Reply Print Delete @ Addresses

FROM: wendy@example.com

TO: josie@example.com

Date Sent: Sept. 28, 2007, 5:22 PM

Dear Josie,

My name is Wendy. I am seven years old. I am in second grade and live in Indiana. The thing I like to do best is ride my bike. My older brother takes me bike riding in the park near my house. Do you like to bike ride?

Write back soon. Tell me all about you!

Wendy

Your Turn

Write an e-mail to a new friend. Tell all about yourself. Tell how old you are, where you live, and what you like to do. Be sure to use complete sentences. Use the Writer's Checklist to check your writing.

Writer's Checklist

☑ **Ideas:** Does my e-mail include important details?

☑ **Word Choice:** Do the words I use show what I am like? Do they tell how I feel?

☑ **Conventions:** Does each sentence have a predicate? Does it tell a complete thought?

☑ **Voice:** Does my writing show that I know who the reader is?

Talk About It

Why do you think many people move to America?

LOG ON Find out more about coming to America at **www.macmillanmh.com**

Coming to America

Vocabulary

patient

practiced

favorite

wrinkled

settled

cuddle

Word Parts

Verbs with the word ending *–ed* tell about actions in the past.

wrinkle – *e* + *ed* = *wrinkled*

My New HOME

by Miguel Vasquez

May 3

We are here in America at last. The airplane trip from Argentina was long. It was hard to be **patient**. I could hardly wait to get here.

I met a boy named Pat on the plane. We spoke both English and Spanish. I told him I had **practiced** my English for years in school. Of all my school subjects, English was my **favorite**. I liked it the best.

May 10

Two days ago we got to our new home. When we went inside I **wrinkled** my nose. I smelled something different. Our neighbor was cooking spicy food.

Now my family is unpacking and getting **settled**. My dad got me a kitten named Carla. When I miss Argentina, I **cuddle** her and hold her close. Then I feel better.

Reread for **Comprehension**

STRATEGY SKILL

Summarize
Make and Confirm Predictions
Summarizing can help you make predictions, or guesses, about what will happen later in the story. Reread the first journal entry and use the chart to make and confirm predictions about what happens in the next entry.

What I Predict	What Happens

Comprehension

Genre
Realistic Fiction is a made-up story that could happen in real life.

Summarize
Make and Confirm Predictions
As you read, use your Predictions Chart.

What I Predict	What Happens

Read to Find Out
How does Yoon feel about her new class?

My Name Is Yoon

by HELEN RECORVITS

illustrated by GABI SWIATKOWSKA

Award
Winning
Illustrator

My name is Yoon. I came here from Korea, a country far away.

It was not long after we **settled** in that my father called me to his side.

"Soon you will go to your new school. You must learn to print your name in English," he said. "Here. This is how it looks."

YOON

I **wrinkled** my nose. I did not like YOON. Lines. Circles. Each standing alone.

"My name looks happy in Korean," I said. "The symbols dance together.

"And in Korean my name means Shining Wisdom. I like the Korean way better."

"Well, you must learn to write it this way. Remember, even when you write in English, it still means Shining Wisdom."

I did not want to learn the new way. I wanted to go back home to Korea. I did not like America. Everything was different here. But my father handed me a pencil, and his eyes said Do-as-I-say. He showed me how to print every letter in the English alphabet. So I **practiced**, and my father was very pleased.

"Look," he called to my mother. "See how well our little Yoon does!"

"Yes," she said. "She will be a wonderful student!"

I wrinkled my nose.

My first day at school I sat quietly at my desk while the teacher talked about CAT. She wrote CAT on the chalkboard. She read a story about CAT. I did not know what her words meant, but I knew what the pictures said. She sang a song about CAT. It was a pretty song, and I tried to sing the words, too.

Later she gave me a paper with my name on it.

"Name. Yoon," she said. And she pointed to the empty lines underneath.

I did not want to write YOON. I wrote CAT instead. I wrote CAT on every line.

CAT CAT CAT

I wanted to be CAT. I wanted to hide in a corner. My mother would find me and **cuddle** up close to me. I would close my eyes and mew quietly.

The teacher looked at my paper. She shook her head and frowned. "So you are CAT?" she asked.

The ponytail girl sitting behind me giggled.

After school I said to my father, "We should go back to Korea. It is better there."

"Do not talk like that," he said. "America is your home now."

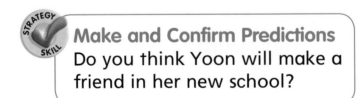

Make and Confirm Predictions
Do you think Yoon will make a friend in her new school?

I sat by the window and watched a little robin hop, hop in the yard. "He is all alone, too," I thought. "He has no friends. No one likes him."

Then I had a very good idea. "If I draw a picture for the teacher, then maybe she will like me."

It was the best bird I had ever drawn. "Look, Father," I said proudly.

"Oh, this makes me happy," he said. "Now do this." And he showed me how to print BIRD under the picture.

The next day at school the teacher handed me another YOON paper to print. But I did not want to print YOON. I wrote BIRD instead. I wrote BIRD on every line.

I wanted to be BIRD. I wanted to fly, fly back to Korea. I would fly to my nest, and I would tuck my head under my little brown wing.

The teacher looked at my paper. Again she shook her head. "So you are BIRD?" she asked.

Then I showed her my special robin drawing. I patted my red dress, and then I patted the red robin. I lowered my head and peeked up at her. The teacher smiled.

"How was school today, my daughter?" my mother asked.

"I think the teacher likes me a little," I said.

"Well, that is good!" my mother said.

"Yes, but at my school in Korea, I was my teacher's **favorite**. I had many friends. Here I am all alone."

"You must be **patient** with everyone, including yourself," my mother said. "You will be a fine student, and you will make many new friends here."

133

The next day at recess, I stood near the fence by myself. I watched the ponytail girl sitting on the swing. She watched me, too. Suddenly she jumped off the swing and ran over to me. She had a package in her hand. The wrapper said CUPCAKE. She opened it and gave me one. She giggled. I giggled, too.

When we were back in school, the teacher gave us more printing papers. I did not want to write YOON. I wrote CUPCAKE instead.

I wanted to be CUPCAKE. The children would clap their hands when they saw me. They would be excited. "CUPCAKE!" they would say. "Here is CUPCAKE!"

The teacher looked at my paper. "And today you are CUPCAKE!" she said. She smiled a very big smile. Her eyes said I-like-this-girl-Yoon.

After school I told my mother about my ponytail friend. I sang a new song for my father. I sang in English.

"You make us so proud, little Yoon," my mother said.

"Maybe America will be a good home," I thought. "Maybe different is good, too."

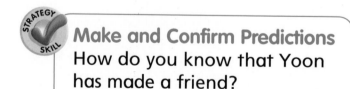

Make and Confirm Predictions
How do you know that Yoon has made a friend?

The next day at school, I could hardly wait to print. And this time I wrote YOON on every line.

When my teacher looked at my paper, she gave me a big hug. "Aha! You are YOON!" she said.

Yes. I am YOON.

I write my name in English now. It still means Shining Wisdom.

Meet the Author and Illustrator

Helen Recorvits began writing stories when she was a young girl. When Helen was a teenager, she wrote for a small newspaper. Today, she is a second-grade teacher as well as a writer. Helen says, "I love writing stories about people."

Gabi Swiatkowska won an award for her illustrations in this book. Gabi went to art school in Poland, and now lives in Brooklyn, New York. She knows what it is like to live in a new country.

Another book illustrated by Gabi Swiatkowska

LOG ON Find out more about Gabi Swiatkowska at **www.macmillanmh.com**

Author's Purpose
Helen Recorvits wanted her words to bring Yoon to life. Write a letter from Yoon to her friends.

Comprehension Check

Retelling Cards

Retell the Story

Use the Retelling Cards to retell the story.

Think and Compare

1. At the beginning of the story, did you think Yoon would like school? How does she feel at the end of the story? **Summarize: Make and Confirm Predictions**

What I Predict	What Happens

2. Reread pages 128–131. Why does Yoon write BIRD on her paper? Use the text to explain. **Analyze**

3. How would you feel if you had to go to a new school in a different country? Explain. **Synthesize**

4. Why do you think Yoon's mother tells her she must be **patient** about her new life in America? **Analyze**

5. Read "My New Home" on pages 114–115. How is Miguel like Yoon? How is he different? **Reading/Writing Across Texts**

New Americans

by Ken Lee

Immigrants have been coming from other **countries** to live in America for many years. Immigrants are people who come to live in one country after they have left another country. Some immigrants come because they have family or friends in America. Others come because they want to work in America.

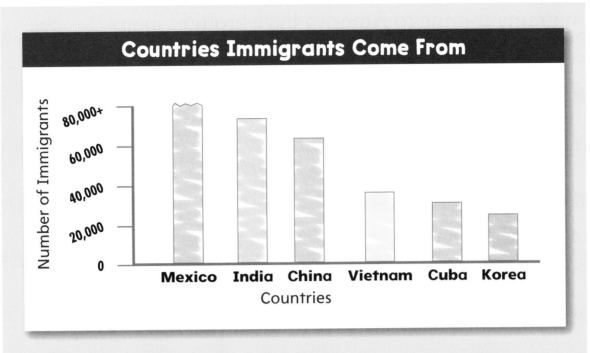

Countries Immigrants Come From

Number of Immigrants

80,000+
60,000
40,000
20,000
0

Mexico India China Vietnam Cuba Korea

Countries

This bar graph shows countries that some immigrants came from in one year. Use the bars to compare how many people came from each of these countries.

Immigrants come to America from many countries around the world. They come from countries as far away as India and Korea. They come from countries as close as Canada and Mexico.

America has a mix of people from all over the world. Because of this, people here have many different backgrounds and **cultures**. They have ideas and ways of life that they share with one another.

Immigrants coming to America have brought many interesting things with them. They have brought wonderful new kinds of music and clothes. Immigrants have also brought new words for people to speak and write. For example, did you know the words *banana* and *poncho* are actually Spanish words?

Many tasty foods that we enjoy have been brought to the United States by immigrants, too. Have you ever eaten an avocado? Avocados came from Mexico. Here they are grown in California and Florida.

Some of the music we listen to came here from other countries. *Reggae* is music from Jamaica. A lot of music and dances that we enjoy are from Cuba.

Immigrants learn many new things from people in America. People in America learn many new things from immigrants.

Rumba dancers

Connect and Compare

1. Which country on the graph shows the most immigrants for one year? **Bar Graphs**

2. Think about this article and *My Name Is Yoon*. Find the country that Yoon came from on the graph. Write about how the number of immigrants compares with the other countries on the graph. **Reading/Writing Across Texts**

Social Studies Activity

Research one of the countries from the graph. Write a paragraph about it.

LOG ON Find out more about immigration at **www.macmillanmh.com**

Write a Journal Entry

July 4

I used different types of sentences in my writing.

What a super day! We went to the beach for my first 4th of July! First Maggie and I made a huge sand castle. Then we collected shiny shells.

I used <u>and</u> to combine sentences that had the same subject.

When it got late, we put on dry clothes and ate our dinner. Then we waited until it was dark for the fireworks. I told Dad that watching sparkling fireworks at the beach is the best!

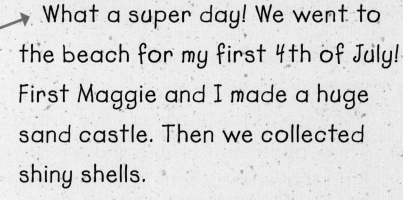

Your Turn

Write a journal entry about something that happened to you. Use lively words to show how you feel. Combine any sentences that have the same predicate. Use the Writer's Checklist to check your writing.

Writer's Checklist

☐ **Sentence Fluency:** Did I vary sentences in my writing? Did I combine sentences?

☑ **Ideas:** Do my sentences tell about my experience?

☑ **Voice:** Did I use lively words to show enthusiasm in my writing?

☑ **Organization:** Did I tell what happened in a way that makes sense?

Test Strategy

Think and Search
The answer is in more than one place. Keep reading to find the answer.

Animal Parents and Their Babies

by Jasmine Brown

All animals have babies. Animal parents have different ways of taking care of their babies. Mammal and bird babies cannot care for themselves right away. They need their parents to keep them safe, warm, and fed.

A mother cat feeds her kittens. Kittens cannot walk until they are three weeks old. ▼

150

Go on ▶

Mammals have backbones and fur or hair. Bears, giraffes, and human beings are all mammals. Most baby mammals do not know how to feed themselves. They depend on others. The mammal mothers feed their babies with milk from their bodies.

When the babies get older, mammal parents teach them to find food. Bear cubs learn to catch fish by watching their mother. Their mother also shows them which berries are good to eat.

Mammal parents keep their babies safe. Young giraffes cannot run fast. An enemy may catch one and eat it. If an enemy attacks, the giraffe parents kick it and scare it away.

A mother giraffe leads its baby to food. ▶

Go on ▶ 151

Most baby birds do not know how to feed themselves. A penguin chick cannot swim or fish for food. So penguin parents work together. One catches fish. The other keeps the chick safe at home. After a while, the chick grows adult feathers. Then it can fish for its own food.

After some time, animal babies become adults. Then they take care of themselves. They may have their own babies, too.

This penguin father feeds his chick. He coughs up food from his stomach. Then he puts it into his chick's mouth. ▶

Go on ▶

Tip

Keep reading.

Directions:
Answer the questions.

1. **How do some animal babies first get food?**

   A   Mammal babies learn to fish.

   B   Their parents feed them.

   C   Bird babies start to swim.

   D   All babies stay helpless.

2. **How do some animal parents care for their babies?**

   A   Giraffes swim with the babies.

   B   Penguins kick their enemy.

   C   They feed them and keep them safe.

   D   They feed fish to the birds.

3. **Look at the photo captions. How are some baby animals fed?**

Writing Prompt

Think about someone who has taken care of you. Write a journal entry about how this person cared for you.

Talk About It

Why do you think people like to grow plants?

LOG ON Find out more about plants at
www.macmillanmh.com

Plants Alive!

Plant Power!

by Bradley Roberts

People use plants in many ways. All around us are objects that come from plants.

Your T-shirt probably started as a cotton plant. The cotton plant has seeds called bolls. Hot weather makes the bolls **burst**. When they break open, a soft fluff of cotton pops out. The fluff sometimes **drifts** in the air, moving slowly in the wind. People can spin the fluff into thread that becomes material.

Other plants are used to make medicines. Some of these plants are found in a dry, hot place like the **desert**. The aloe plant has a juice that helps heal cuts. Many people grow aloe plants. An aloe plant **drowns** easily. It is important not to give them too much water because they will die. To get the aloe juice, **gently** break off a leaf. Do it carefully to not harm the plant.

Some plants are so big that we can build with them. Many houses are made from trees. Look at the houses of the people who live near you. Does your **neighbor** have a wooden house?

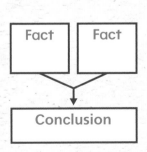

Reread for **Comprehension**

Summarize
Draw Conclusions

After you summarize this article, you can use the summary and what you know from real life to draw conclusions. Reread the article and use the chart to draw conclusions about why plants are important to humans.

Fact	Fact

Conclusion

Comprehension

Genre
An **Informational Story** is a made-up story that gives information about a topic.

 Summarize

Draw Conclusions
As you read, use your Conclusion Chart.

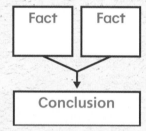

```
[Fact]  [Fact]
        ↓
   [Conclusion]
```

Read to Find Out
What does the tiny seed need to grow?

Eric Carle

The Tiny Seed

It is Autumn.

A strong wind is blowing. It blows flower seeds
high in the air and carries them far across
the land. One of the seeds is tiny,
smaller than any of the others.
Will it be able to keep up with the others?
And where are they all going?

One of the seeds flies higher than the others.
Up, up it goes! It flies too high and the sun's rays
burn it up. But the tiny seed sails on with the others.

Draw Conclusions
Besides the sun, what other
dangers may the seeds find?

Another seed lands on a tall and icy mountain.
The ice never melts, and the seed cannot grow.
The rest of the seeds fly on. But the tiny seed
does not go as fast as the others.

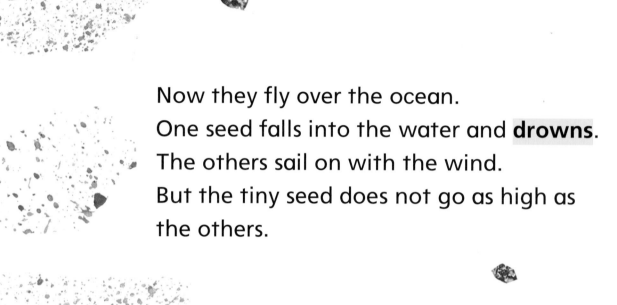

Now they fly over the ocean.
One seed falls into the water and **drowns**.
The others sail on with the wind.
But the tiny seed does not go as high as
the others.

One seed **drifts** down onto the **desert**.
It is hot and dry, and the seed cannot grow.
Now the tiny seed is flying very low,
but the wind pushes it on with the others.

Finally the wind stops and the seeds fall **gently**
down on the ground. A bird comes by
and eats one seed. The tiny seed is not eaten.
It is so small that the bird does not see it.

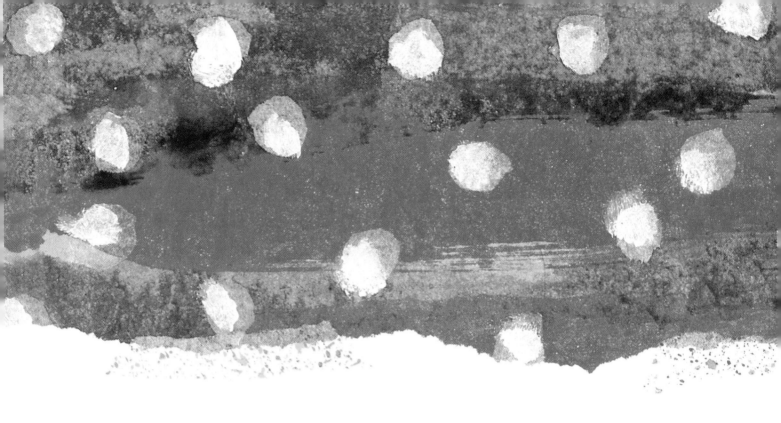

Now it is Winter.

After their long trip the seeds settle down.
They look just as if they are going to sleep
in the earth. Snow falls and covers them
like a soft white blanket. A hungry mouse
that also lives in the ground eats a seed
for his lunch. But the tiny seed lies very still
and the mouse does not see it.

Now it is Spring.

After a few months the snow has melted.
It is really Spring! Birds fly by. The sun shines.
Rain falls. The seeds grow so round and full
they start to **burst** open a little. Now they
are not seeds any more. They are plants.
First they send roots down into the earth.
Then their little stems and leaves begin to grow
up toward the sun and air. There is another plant
that grows much faster than the new little
plants. It is a big fat weed. And it takes all
the sunlight and the rain away from one of
the small new plants. And that little plant dies.

The tiny seed hasn't begun to grow yet.
It will be too late! Hurry!
But finally it too starts to grow into a plant.

The warm weather also brings the children out to play. They too have been waiting for the sun and spring time. One child doesn't see the plants as he runs along and—Oh! He breaks one! Now it cannot grow any more.

The tiny plant that grew from the tiny seed is growing fast, but its **neighbor** grows even faster. Before the tiny plant has three leaves the other plant has seven! And look! A bud! And now even a flower!

But what is happening? First there are footsteps.
Then a shadow looms over them. Then a hand
reaches down and breaks off the flower.
A boy has picked the flower to give to a friend.

It is Summer.

Now the tiny plant from the tiny seed
is all alone. It grows on and on. It doesn't stop.
The sun shines on it and the rain waters it.
It has many leaves. It grows taller and taller.
It is taller than the people. It is taller than
the trees. It is taller than the houses.
And now a flower grows on it. People come
from far and near to look at this flower.
It is the tallest flower they have ever seen.
It is a giant flower.

174

All summer long the birds and bees and butterflies come visiting. They have never seen such a big and beautiful flower.

Now it is Autumn again.

The days grow shorter. The nights grow cooler.
And the wind carries yellow and red leaves
past the flower. Some petals drop from the
giant flower and they sail along with the bright
leaves over the land and down to the ground.

Draw Conclusions
What do you think will
happen to the flower?

The wind blows harder. The flower has lost almost all of its petals. It sways and bends away from the wind. But the wind grows stronger and shakes the flower. Once more the wind shakes the flower, and this time the flower's seed pod opens. Out come many tiny seeds that quickly sail far away on the wind.

Cut, Paste, and Learn with Eric Carle

Eric Carle has illustrated more than 70 books. He wrote most of these books, too. Many books, such as *The Tiny Seed*, are about nature.

Eric's artwork is called *collage*. First, he paints on paper. Then he cuts it into small shapes. He glues the painted paper in layers to make the larger shapes he wants.

Eric says, "I want to show [children] that learning is really both fascinating and fun."

Other books written and illustrated by Eric Carle

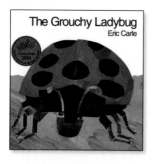

 LOG ON Find out more about Eric Carle at **www.macmillanmh.com**

Author's Purpose

Eric Carle wants to teach readers about nature. Think about a flower, plant, or tree. Describe what it looks like and how it changes.

182

Comprehension Check

Retell the Story

Use the Retelling Cards to retell the story.

Retelling Cards

Think and Compare

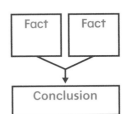

1. How does being very small help the tiny seed?
Summarize: Draw Conclusions

2. Reread page 174. How does being all alone in summer help the tiny plant? **Analyze**

3. What new information did you learn about plants and seeds from the story? What did you know already? Explain. **Evaluate**

4. Why does the story end with the flower making new seeds? What do you think will happen to the new seeds? **Synthesize**

5. "Plant Power!" on pages 156–157 tells about how cotton bolls **burst**. Based on what you learned in *The Tiny Seed*, how do you think cotton seeds are spread? **Reading/Writing Across Texts**

Plant Parts

by Pilar Jacob

A plant is a living thing. It uses its many parts to grow from a small **seed** to a large plant. Each part helps the plant stay healthy. Plants also need **sunlight** to grow. They get light from the sun and **minerals** from the soil. These things help the plant stay alive and grow.

Flowers
Flowers make seeds that can grow into new plants.

Stem
The stem helps hold the plant up. It moves the food and water from the roots to the other parts of the plant.

Leaves
Leaves use sunlight, water, and air to make food.

Roots
A plant grows roots under the ground. The roots hold the plant in place.

Fruit
Some plants have fruit. The fruit grows around the seeds and keeps them safe.

Seeds
Seeds can grow into new plants.

Connect and Compare

1. What are two ways that roots help a plant stay alive? **Diagrams and Labels**

2. Look at the picture of the giant flower at the end of the *The Tiny Seed*. Draw a picture that looks like this flower. Label each of the plant parts. **Reading/Writing Across Texts**

 ### Science Activity

Research a plant that grows fruit. Make a diagram of this plant and label each part.

 Find more about plants at **www.macmillanmh.com**

Write About How to Do Something

I drew a picture of nouns to show what is needed.

I wrote important details. Each step is numbered to show the correct order.

How to Grow Marigolds

You will need marigold seeds, a pot with soil, and water.

marigold seeds   pot with soil   water

1. Make two holes in the soil about two inches apart. Make each hole one inch deep.
2. Put two seeds in each hole. Cover the seeds with soil.
3. Put the pot in a sunny place.
4. Water it about every four days. Watch your marigolds grow!

Your Turn

Make a poster about how to do something. Include important details. Use exact nouns to tell all the things you need. Draw pictures with labels to show what you need. Number the steps to show the correct order. Use the Writer's Checklist to check your work.

Writer's Checklist

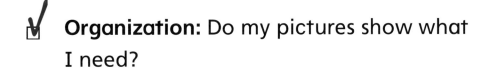

☑ **Ideas:** Is my topic clear and easy to understand? Did I include important details?

✓ **Organization:** Do my pictures show what I need?

✓ **Organization:** Did I number the steps to show the correct order?

✓ **Conventions:** Did I label the nouns in my pictures?

Animal Rescue

Talk About It

How do people help animals that are sick or injured?

LOG ON Find out more about animal rescue at **www.macmillanmh.com**

Vocabulary

young

examines

mammal

normal

hunger

rescued

Context Clues

Antonyms are words that have opposite meanings.

Young and *old* are antonyms.

A WHALE IS SAVED!

by Elizabeth Baker

A **young** whale got stuck in Drew Harbor today. The whale was small and had been born recently. Some people saw the whale in trouble. They called the police.

Soon help was on the way. Jenny Litz arrived first. She is a scientist who **examines** whales.

Jenny looks at every part of an animal to see if it is healthy. A whale is a **mammal**. Mammals are warm-blooded animals that have hair and drink their mother's milk. Jenny checked the whale's heartbeat and breathing. She said the whale seemed **normal**. There were no signs of illness.

Next, Jenny checked to see if **hunger** was a problem. Going a long time without food can be dangerous for a whale. But this whale seemed healthy and well fed.

The helpers acted fast. They kept the animal wet. The tide slowly came in. The water got deeper. Soon the whale could swim again. At last, the whale was **rescued**! Its life was saved by Jenny and the other helpers.

Reread for **Comprehension**

Summarize
Sequence
One way to summarize an article is to explain the sequence, or order, of the important events you read about. Reread the article and use the chart to understand what happens first, next, and last in the article.

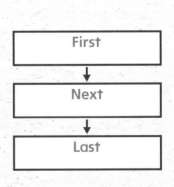

First
↓
Next
↓
Last

Comprehension

Genre
Nonfiction may be a retelling of a true event.

Summarize
Sequence
As you read, use your Sequence Chart.

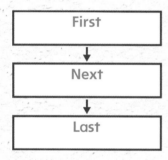

Read to Find Out
How is Sidney found, helped, and released to her ocean home?

A Harbor Seal Pup Grows Up

by Joan Hewett

photographs by Richard Hewett

By the Ocean

The harbor seal pup is 2 weeks old.
Her name is Sidney. Sidney stays close to
her mother. She drinks her mother's milk.

Waves crash on the rocky beach. Harbor
seal families lie in the warm sun.

Sidney and her mother lie in the sun too.

Sidney's mother gets hungry. She dives in the
water to catch fish. The water is too cold for
Sidney. So Sidney stays on the shore.

The seal pup waits for her mother. She
waits for 3 days. She is very hungry.

People notice the seal pup. She is alone.
Will her mother come back?

The next day, the pup is still alone. The people call for help. Sidney is **rescued**.

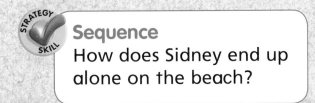

Sequence
How does Sidney end up alone on the beach?

Nursed Back to Health

Sidney is brought to a sea **mammal** center.

A scientist named Peter is in charge. Peter takes care of **young** seals. He lifts the thin pup from her cage.

Sidney is weak from **hunger**. Peter knows just what to do. He puts a tube in Sidney's mouth.

Then Nicole pumps a drink into Sidney's stomach. The drink is like a mother seal's milk.

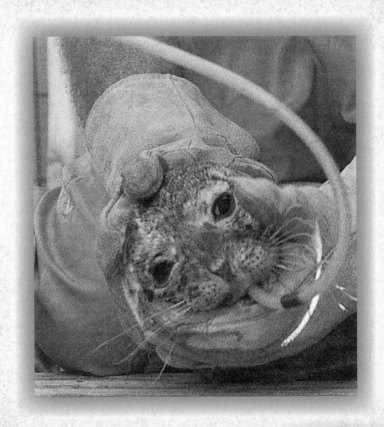

Sidney is full. She is also very tired.
She falls asleep.

When Sidney wakes up, her eyes are bright. She looks around.

Peter **examines** the pup. Her heartbeat is **normal**. So is her temperature. She is healthy.

Sidney has a full set of teeth. That means she is at least 3 weeks old. Sidney is small for her age.

Sidney gets her drink 3 times a day. She becomes stronger. Using her flippers, she scoots around.

A child's plastic pool becomes Sidney's playpen. She likes the water. She swims faster and faster.

Nicole shows Sidney a fish. Sidney does not want it.

Nicole does not give up. Day after day, she wiggles a fish in front of Sidney. Then one day, the pup swallows it.

Before long, Sidney wants to eat fish. She waits for her bucket of fish in the morning.

The pup is gaining weight. She no longer needs her healthy drink.

Sidney is 5 weeks old. She has a thick layer of fat. The fat will keep her warm in cold water.

Sidney is ready to be on her own.

Sequence
What steps are taken to help Sidney at the sea mammal center?

Returning to the Ocean

Peter puts the pup in a carrying case. Other
scientists take over. They carry Sidney onto
a boat. Sidney is excited by the ocean's salty
smell. She shakes the case.

The boat heads toward an island. When they are almost there, the boat stops. It is time to say good-bye.

A scientist tips the case. "Good luck, little one," she says.

Sidney slips into the water. She will
find other seals. She will catch fish.
Sidney will grow up in her ocean home.

Joan and Richard Hewett's Animal Adventures

Joan Hewett and her husband **Richard Hewett** created their first children's book in 1977. After that, Richard says, "I knew that this was what I wanted to do. Children's books are the best."

Joan and Richard have worked on more than 20 children's books together. Joan says, "We always enjoy doing books that bring us in close contact with animals. Still, photographing harbor seals and other wild animals takes patience. It's a challenge, and that's part of the fun."

Other books by Joan Hewett and Richard Hewett

 Find out more about Joan Hewett and Richard Hewett at **www.macmillanmh.com**

Author's Purpose

Joan and Richard Hewett wrote this book to show how animals sometimes need our help. Think about a time when you helped an animal or a person. Write about what you did.

Comprehension Check

Retell the Story

Use the Retelling Cards to retell the selection.

Retelling Cards

Think and Compare

1. What happened to Sidney at the beginning, the middle, and the end of the selection? **Summarize: Sequence**

```
┌─────────────┐
│    First    │
└─────────────┘
       ↓
┌─────────────┐
│    Next     │
└─────────────┘
       ↓
┌─────────────┐
│    Last     │
└─────────────┘
```

2. Reread pages 196–198. Sidney was very thin when she was **rescued**. Use the text to explain why. **Analyze**

3. How do you think the scientists felt when they said good-bye to Sidney? Explain. **Evaluate**

4. Why do you think the scientists brought Sidney back to the ocean after she got healthy? **Analyze**

5. How is Sidney like the whale in "A Whale Is Saved" on pages 190–191? **Reading/Writing Across Texts**

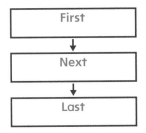

Poetry

Genre
Poems can describe things in interesting or unusual ways.

SKILL ✓

Literary Element
Similes compare one thing to another. A simile uses the words *like* or *as*. Similes help readers picture what something looks, sounds, or feels like.

The Puppy

Anonymous

Call the puppy,
And give him some milk.
Brush his coat
Till it shines like silk.
Call the dog
And give him a bone.
Go for a walk,
Then take him home.

Connect and Compare

1. What things are compared in the poem? How can you tell that the comparison is a simile? **Simile**

2. Think about how the scientists cared for Sidney in *A Harbor Seal Pup Grows Up*. How is caring for a seal pup like caring for a puppy or a dog? How is it different? **Reading/Writing Across Texts**

 Find out more about animal care at **www.macmillanmh.com**

Important Details
A good writer uses **important details** to make information clear.

Write About How to Care for an Animal

How to Care for Fred
by Kim S.

1. Feed Fred two small cans of food each day.

   cat food →

I gave details about the water so the information was clear.

2. Give Fred fresh water each day.

   fresh water →

I added an "s" to make <u>day</u> plural.

3. Brush Fred every two days.

   cat brush →

4. Give Fred lots of love.

   love ♥ →

Your Turn

Think about an animal you take care of. It may be your pet or the pet of someone you know. Write a numbered list that tells how to care for it. Then draw a picture with labels to show each noun. Use the Writer's Checklist to check your writing.

Writer's Checklist

☑ **Ideas:** Are my ideas clear? Did I pay attention to important details?

☑ **Word Choice:** Did I use exact words that make it clear how to care for the animal?

☑ **Conventions:** Do my sentences use plural nouns correctly?

☑ **Conventions:** Did I use a capital letter to begin each sentence?

A Hospital Visit

Vocabulary

serious
broken
personal
informs
heal

Paramedics come when someone is sick or hurt.

A Ride to Help

The lights flash and the sirens scream. An ambulance is on its way. There is a **serious** problem. Someone is hurt or very sick.

Paramedics drive the ambulance. They also give help to people on the way to the hospital. Inside the ambulance are medical supplies. If someone has a **broken** bone, the paramedics use special tools to keep it still.

Paramedics take a **personal** interest in helping people. They give aid and get people to the hospital as quickly as possible.

220

Time for an X-Ray

Who needs an X-ray? People who have broken a bone will usually get an X-ray taken at the hospital. An X-ray is a special kind of photograph that shows bones and other parts inside the body.

What happens when you get an X-ray? First, an X-ray worker takes the picture. Then, a doctor looks at the X-ray to find out if a bone is broken. Last, the doctor **informs** the patient about how the bone will **heal**. She may tell the patient that he or she needs a cast. The doctor also explains that the bone will mend over time.

LOG ON Visit a hospital at
www.macmillanmh.com

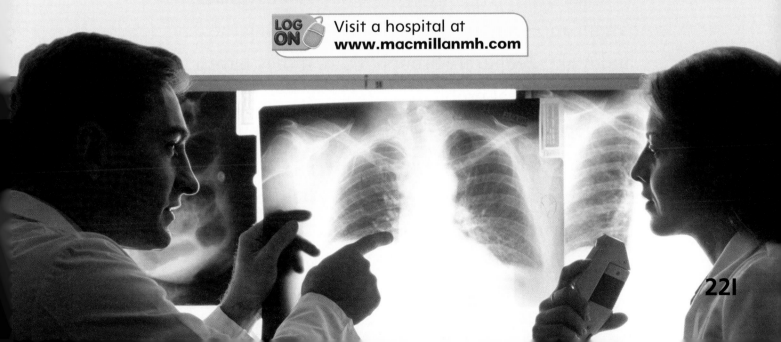

A Trip to the Emergency Room

Who works in the emergency room?

Oh, no! You have a **broken** bone. Where do you go? To the hospital emergency room, of course. The emergency room can be a busy place. Ambulances and people arrive there during the day and night. People are brought there if they have a **serious** medical problem.

Doctors and nurses work in the emergency room. Their job is to help people who are sick or hurt. Other people work there, too. They help keep the hospital running properly. Let's meet some of the people who work in a hospital emergency room.

222

H Admissions Worker

The first person you see in the emergency room is an admissions worker. The hospital needs to keep track of the patients coming into the emergency room. The admissions person checks you in. The adult who is with you will fill out hospital forms. The forms ask for your **personal** information and why you came to the hospital.

Next, a nurse will help you. A nurse's job is to find out about your injury and ask you questions about your health. The nurse will take your temperature and blood pressure and record this information on a chart. The nurse **informs** other people in the hospital about your problem.

Then you will meet an orderly, or nurse's aide. That person will help you get around in the hospital. She will take you to the correct department if you need to get tests done. She may use a wheelchair to take you from one area to another.

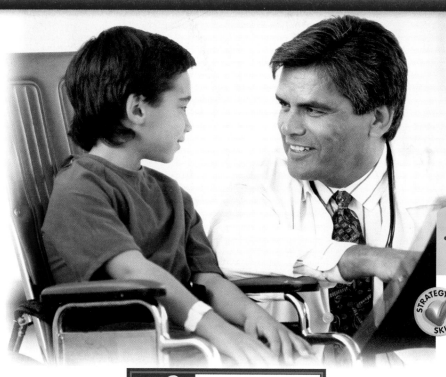

Doctor

Last, it's time for the doctor to examine you. The doctor checks your injury. He also looks at your chart. He arranges for you to get an X-ray if you need one. The doctor knows how to fix your broken bone. He will probably put on a cast so the bone will **heal**. The doctor also decides whether you need to stay in the hospital or if you can go home right away.

So, don't worry if you need to go to the emergency room. Now you know about the people who work there and how they will help you feel better.

Think and Compare

1. Name the people you see in the hospital emergency room in the order you meet them. Use the words *first*, *next*, and *last*.

2. Why does the hospital need an admissions worker?

3. Have you ever gone to the hospital or the emergency room? If yes, tell about it. If no, tell about a time you went to the doctor.

4. How are paramedics similar to doctors? How are they different?

225

A Visit to the Dentist

You need your teeth to eat. To take good care of them, eat healthful foods, and remember to brush and floss every day. It's also important to visit the dentist every six months.

Here's what happens at a dental checkup. First, the dentist takes X-rays. These pictures of your teeth show if you have any cavities. They also show the health of your teeth and gums. Next, the dentist or an assistant cleans your teeth and makes them shine.

Last, the dentist looks carefully inside your mouth. He or she uses a little mirror to see the teeth in the back of your mouth. The dentist is pleased when your teeth and gums are healthy! In six months it will be time to come back for another checkup.

Go On ▶

Directions: Answer the questions.

1. What can you learn from your dentist?

A   how to read X-rays

B   how to become a dentist

C   the best way to chew your food

D   how to take good care of your teeth

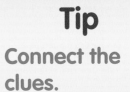

Tip
Connect the clues.

2. Why do dentists look inside your mouth?

A   to see if you eat healthful foods

B   to check the X-rays

C   to look for problems

D   to see if your teeth are clean

3. How is this article written?

A   It tells events in order.

B   It describes what something looks like.

C   It compares two things.

D   It shows you how to make something.

4. Why might a dentist give you a new toothbrush?

5. Why do you think it is important to go to a dentist every six months? Use details from the selection in your answer.

Write to a Prompt

Write about a worker who has helped you. Your story should be between one and four paragraphs long.

Help at the Library

I went to the library last summer. There were so many books! I asked the librarian for help.

First, Ms. Valdez asked me what I liked to read. I said I liked both made-up stories and true stories. Next, Ms. Valdez helped me find two good books. One was fiction, about a talking cat. The other book was nonfiction. It was about a paramedic.

Last, I took the books home. They were both fun to read. Now I always ask Ms. Valdez for help at the library. She really knows how to find the right books for me.

I put the events in order to organize my writing.

Your Writing Prompt

Think of a time when a worker helped you. Tell how you felt about the person and how he or she helped you. Tell what happened first, next, and last. Your story should be two or three paragraphs long.

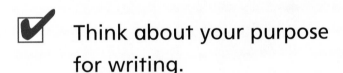

Writer's Checklist

☑ Think about your purpose for writing.

☑ Plan your writing before beginning.

☑ Make sure your story has a clear sequence.

☑ Use your best spelling, grammar, and punctuation.

229

How
Animals
GROW

Leo Grows Up

by Kevin Lee

Leo was a playful kitten. He loved to chase and play with his friends. But sometimes the other kittens weren't nice.

"Look at Leo," they said. "Why is he so big?" The kittens **giggled**. Leo heard their laughs, and it made him sad.

Once a bird **fluttered** by him, flapping its wings as it passed by.

"I wish I was like a bird," said Leo. "I would be light and tiny."

Leo left the kittens. He explored the jungle on his own for many months. Leo grew taller. His fur became thicker.

One day Leo heard a roar behind a bush. He stopped and **peered** over it. When he looked over the top, Leo saw animals that he **recognized**. He knew he had seen them before. They looked just like him, but bigger!

The giant cats ran away. They **vanished** into the trees so Leo couldn't see them anymore. He ran after them. "Look! Another lion," one of the big cats said.

Then Leo knew why he was bigger than the other kittens. He was a lion, not a cat! That night Leo **snuggled** with the other lions. They slept close together. Finally, Leo belonged.

Reread for **Comprehension**

Ask Questions
Make Inferences
Asking questions can help you understand what you are reading. You can ask yourself about what the author tells you and use what you already know to make an inference about a character. Reread the story and use the chart to make inferences about Leo.

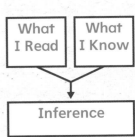

What I Read	What I Know

Inference

Comprehension

Genre
Fantasy is a story that has made-up characters, settings, or other things that could not happen in real life.

Ask Questions
Make Inferences
As you read, use your Inference Chart.

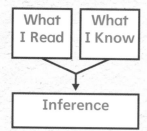

Read to Find Out
How do you know Farfallina and Marcel are good friends?

Farfallina & Marcel

by Holly Keller

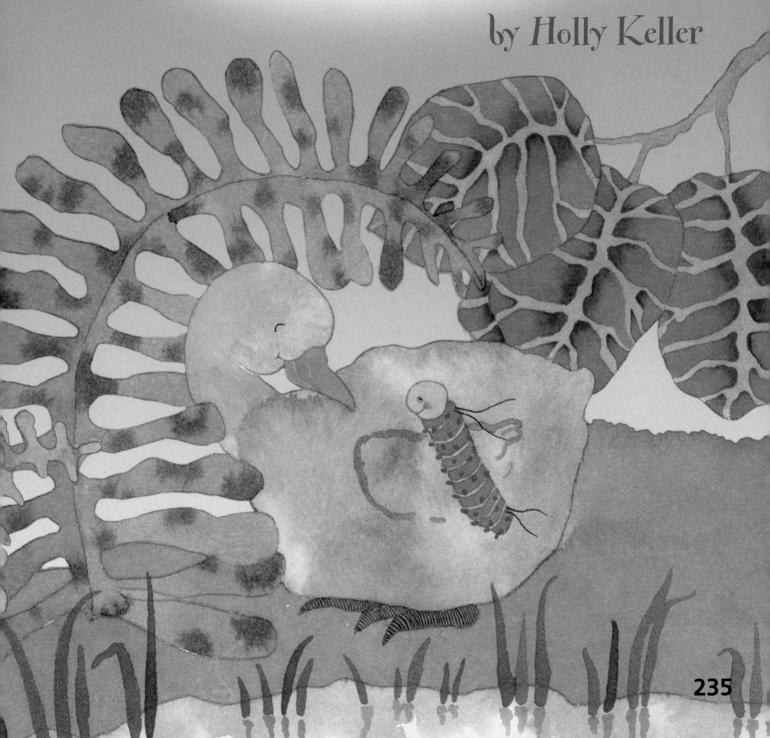

The rain fell all morning.
It splattered on the pond and
splashed on Farfallina's leaf.
She found a dry spot and ate it.
"Hey," said a little voice.
"You're eating my umbrella."
Farfallina **peered** over the edge.
A small gray bird was huddled underneath.

Farfallina liked his soft feathers and his gentle eyes.

"I'm Farfallina," she said,

and she slid down to the ground.

"My name is Marcel," said the bird.

He liked Farfallina's smile and her pretty colors.

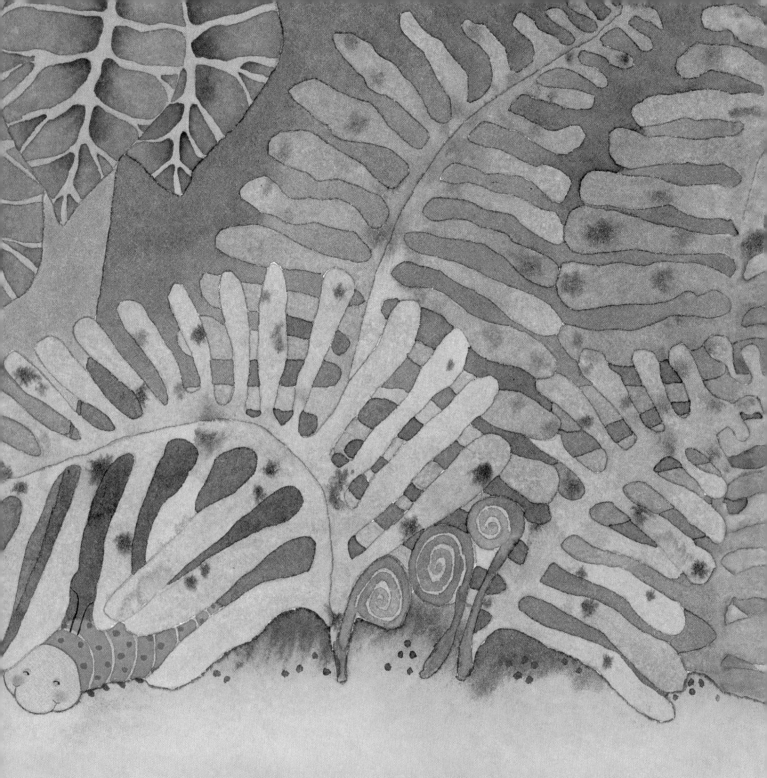

The rain turned to drizzle, and Farfallina wanted to play.
"I'll hide and you find me," she said.
Marcel agreed.
Farfallina hid under a fern close to the ground
because she knew that Marcel couldn't climb.

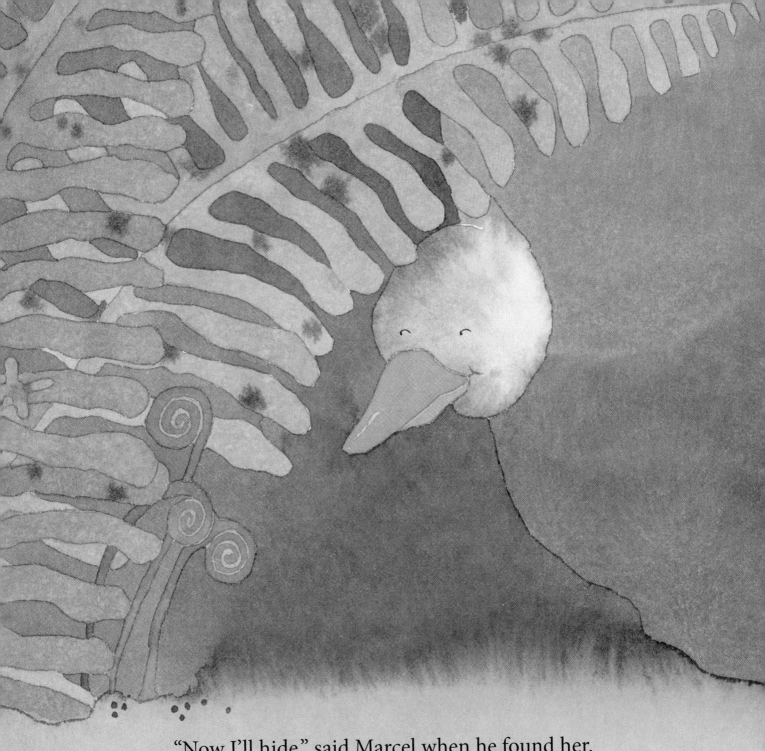

"Now I'll hide," said Marcel when he found her.
And he hid right behind the tree
because he knew that Farfallina moved slowly.

Make Inferences
How do you think Farfallina and Marcel feel about each other. Why?

"I can take you for a ride on the pond," said Marcel.
Farfallina inched her way up to Marcel's back.
"You tickle," said Marcel, and he slipped into the water.

Farfallina **giggled**.
"There's so much to see," she said.

Farfallina and Marcel played together every day.
They liked the same games, and they liked each other.

But one day Farfallina was not herself.

"I'm not sick," she told Marcel, "just a little uncomfortable.

I need to climb up onto a branch and rest for a while."

"I'll wait for you," Marcel called as Farfallina made

her way up the tree.

Marcel watched until Farfallina was completely

out of sight. Then he settled himself in the grass

and waited.

Night came and then morning,
but Farfallina didn't come down.
Marcel called to her, but she didn't answer.
He was very worried and terribly lonely.

Weeks went by.
The afternoons grew longer and warmer,
and Marcel went to the pond.

He was growing, and when he looked
at his reflection in the water,
he hardly **recognized** himself.

He went back to the tree every day to look
for Farfallina, but she was never there.
And after a while he gave up.

At the top of the tree Farfallina was **snuggled**
in a blanket of glossy silk.
She was growing too.

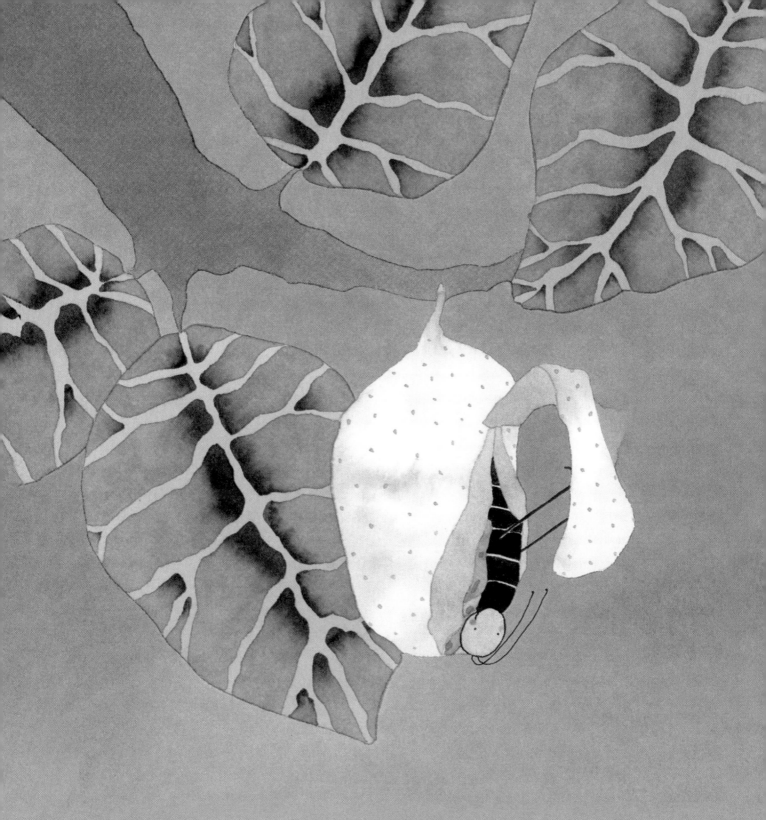

The sky was blue and clear the morning she was ready
to come out and open her beautiful new wings.

She had no idea how long she had been up in the tree, and she floated down to find Marcel.

"I'll just wait," said Farfallina when she didn't see him, and she sat on a flower.

Night came and then morning, but Marcel wasn't there. Farfallina was tired and confused.

She **fluttered** around a bit and went to the pond.

Make Inferences
Why does Farfallina need to spend time alone in the tree?

The pond was glassy smooth
except for the ripples
made by a large, handsome goose
who was swimming in solitary circles.
Farfallina shivered with disappointment.

She went to the pond every day to look for the
small gray bird named Marcel, but he never came.
One morning the goose stopped his silent rounds
and spoke to her.

"You must like it here," he said.

Farfallina fluttered a bit.

"I've been waiting for a friend," she said sadly,

"but I don't think he'll come."

Marcel liked her smile and her brilliant colors.
"I know how you feel," he said. "I lost a friend too.
She just **vanished** into thin air."
Farfallina liked his sleek feathers and his gentle eyes.

"A ride around the pond might cheer you up,"
Marcel said.
Farfallina thought it would, and she settled
herself on Marcel's back.

"It's funny," Marcel said, "but I feel as though
I've known you a long time."
"I was just thinking the same thing," said Farfallina.
"My name is Farfallina. What's yours?"

Marcel stopped suddenly.

He beat the water with his strong wings.

Then he swam round and round and round.

"It's me Farfallina," he shouted. "It's me, Marcel!
Is that really you?"

"It is," Farfallina shouted back.

They looked at each other and laughed.

By evening they had explained everything,
and they fell asleep smiling at the stars.

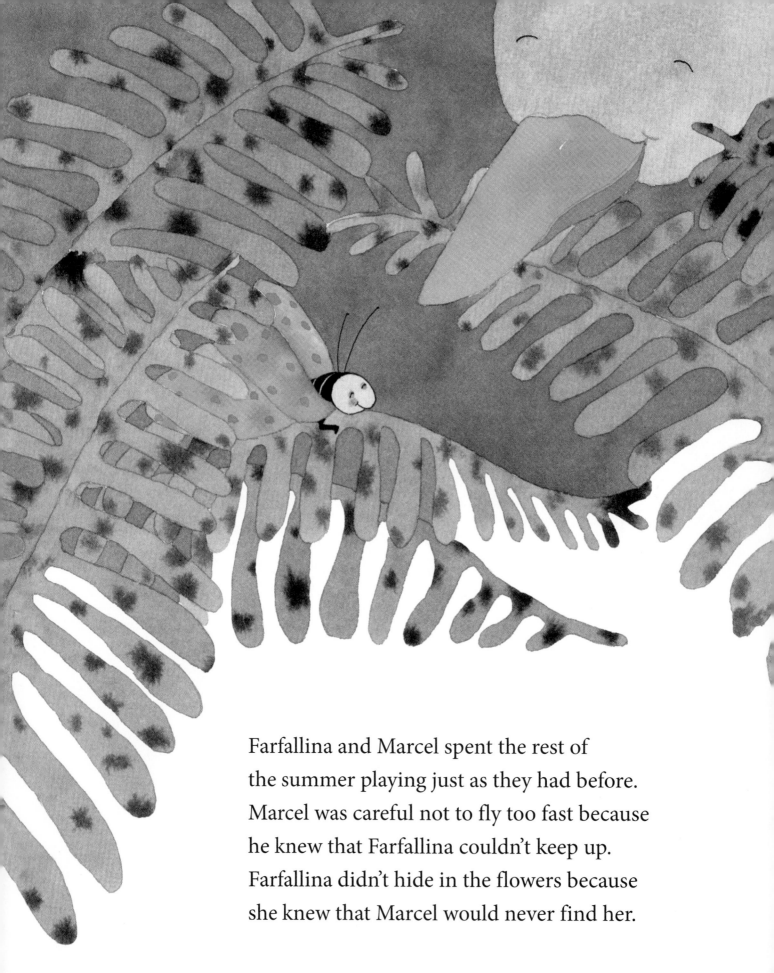

Farfallina and Marcel spent the rest of
the summer playing just as they had before.
Marcel was careful not to fly too fast because
he knew that Farfallina couldn't keep up.
Farfallina didn't hide in the flowers because
she knew that Marcel would never find her.

And when the leaves on the trees
around the pond turned red and gold,
they decided to go south.

Together.

Meet the Author

Holly Keller writes and illustrates books. Her ideas for books come from many places. The idea for *Farfallina and Marcel* started with the word *farfallina*. *Farfallina* means "little butterfly" in Italian. "For some reason," Holly says, "the word caught my fancy."

Other books written and illustrated by Holly Keller

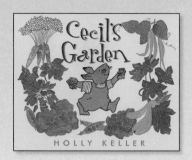

LOG ON Find out more about Holly Keller at **www.macmillanmh.com**

Author's Purpose

Holly Keller wrote this story about good friends for readers to enjoy. Write about two good friends. Tell what they do together.

Comprehension Check

Retell the Story

Use the Retelling Cards to retell the story.

Retelling Cards

Think and Compare

1. Why do you think Marcel is lonely when Farfallina doesn't come back? **Ask Questions: Make Inferences**

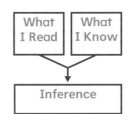

What I Read	What I Know

Inference

2. Reread page 243. Why does Marcel say he hardly **recognized** himself? Use the text and illustration to explain. **Analyze**

3. Would you want a friend like Farfallina or Marcel? Why or why not? **Evaluate**

4. What can you learn about being a good friend from the story? **Analyze**

5. What is similar about the characters in "Leo Grows Up" and *Farfallina and Marcel?* **Reading/Writing Across Texts**

Genre
Nonfiction gives information and facts about a topic.

Text Features
Illustrations are drawings that help readers understand information.

Captions explain what is shown in the illustrations.

Content Words
patterns
stages
hatches

Monarch

Butterflies

Butterflies come in all shapes and sizes. Some are big and some are small. Some have bright spots and some have other markings like dark **patterns** on their wings.

The Monarch and the Skipper are two kinds of butterflies. The Monarch is bigger and more colorful than the Skipper. The Monarch is bright orange and black. It has white spots. The Skipper is brown and has clear spots.

Although these two butterflies look different, they have the same body parts as all other butterflies.

Butterfly Body Parts

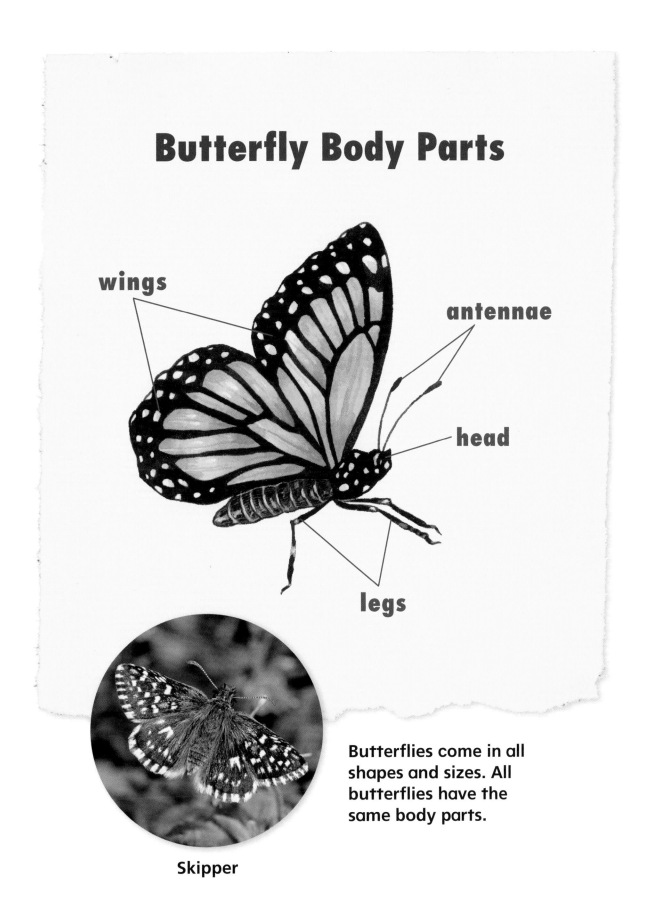

wings

antennae

head

legs

Skipper

Butterflies come in all shapes and sizes. All butterflies have the same body parts.

259

How Butterflies Grow and Change

All butterflies become adults in the same way. Every butterfly's life has four steps, or **stages**, of development.

Stage 1: Egg

A butterfly begins life as an egg. The egg is about the size of the top of a pin. It is usually laid on a leaf. The egg is sticky, so it stays on the leaf.

Stage 2: Larva

When the egg **hatches**, a caterpillar comes out. This part of the butterfly's life is called the larva stage. When the caterpillar is large enough, it hooks itself onto a leaf or branch.

Stage 3: Pupa

The caterpillar makes a hard shell or case to live in. It usually stays inside the shell for a few weeks. This is called the pupa stage. Inside the shell, the caterpillar grows and changes.

Stage 4: Adult

When the shell breaks open, the caterpillar has completely changed into a butterfly. This is the adult stage. After its wings are dry, the butterfly is ready to fly away.

Connect and Compare

1. Reread page 259. What is the same about all butterflies? **Illustrations and Captions**

2. Think about this article and *Farfallina and Marcel*. Explain why Marcel does not know who Farfallina is. Use the names of at least three of the stages of a butterfly's life in your answer. **Reading/Writing Across Texts**

 Science Activity

Use an encyclopedia to research two types of butterflies that live in your state. Tell how they are alike and different.

Find out more about how animals grow at **www.macmillanmh.com**

Writer's Craft

Vary Words
Good writers **vary** the words they choose to make their messages clear.

I added an apostrophe to the end of the word <u>parents</u> to make it possessive.

I used a few different words to describe my new dog.

22 SW 132 Place
Evanston, IL 60060
February 5, 20--

Dear Max,

It was nice to see you at my birthday party. My parents' gift was the best! The puppy they gave me has grown so much. At first Murphy slept in my bed. Now he is too big and has to sleep on the floor. Murphy's snoring sometimes keeps me awake. He is also getting heavy. Soon I won't be able to pick him up.

Your friend,
Carlos

Your Turn

Write a letter to a friend that tells about something new in your life. Vary the words that describe what is new. Use the Writer's Checklist to check your writing.

Writer's Checklist

☑ **Word Choice:** Did I **vary** the words I used?

☑ **Ideas:** Does my letter give details and examples about something new?

☑ **Conventions:** Is my punctuation correct? If I made a plural noun possessive, did I use only an apostrophe?

☑ **Conventions:** Does my letter have all the right parts?

Staying Fit

Talk About It

Playing a sport is one way to stay fit. What are some other ways you like to be active?

LOG ON Find out more about staying fit at **www.macmillanmh.com**

Vocabulary

tryouts

coach

practices

uniform

imaginary

starting

Dictionary

Multiple-meaning words are words that have more than one meaning.

Cinderella took a *coach* with four horses to the ball.

Our baseball *coach* taught us new plays.

Brian Gets Fit on the Field

by Emily Goldman

Brian wanted to be on the school baseball team more than anything. First he had to win a spot on the team. That meant doing his best at **tryouts**. He would have to prove he was an important player for the team.

The school **coach** helped the players learn about baseball. She would decide who would play each position. To do this, the coach held **practices** every day. The students exercised and tried different baseball plays. This helped them become better players. Brian thought it also helped him get in shape. He had never been able to run so far or so fast before.

266

Brian liked the team **uniform**. Each player on the team wore the same clothing: a dark blue shirt and white pants. "I want to wear that uniform," Brian said to his friend Sue. "But I keep thinking something bad will happen. Maybe I will fall or make a bad play."

"Close your eyes and pretend that you are in an **imaginary** game," said Sue. "Maybe that will help."

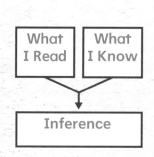

At tryouts, Brian was ready. When he was up at bat, *Crack!* Brian hit the ball very far. He had done his best. Brian knew the coach would let him be a **starting** player. He would get to play in every game!

Reread for **Comprehension**

Ask Questions
Make Inferences
Asking questions about a story and using what you already know can help you figure out something, or make an inference, about a character. Reread the story and use the chart to help you make inferences about Brian.

What I Read	What I Know

Inference

Comprehension

Genre
Realistic Fiction is a made-up story that could happen in real life.

Ask Questions
Make Inferences
As you read, use your Inference Chart.

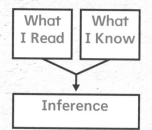

What I Read

What I Know

Inference

Read to Find Out
Explain why you think baseball is important to Emma.

There's Nothing Like BASEBALL

by Angela Johnson

illustrated by Eric Velasquez

Even before I could hold a bat or a glove, I loved baseball. I would sit in the sunshine and soft grass with my best friend, Jamal. Sometimes his cousin Nikki sat with us, too. I always knew that I'd play baseball.

Baseball was coming when the ice dripped drops from the roof.

Baseball was coming when the tulips in the park poked through the ground.

Then, baseball was here. My brother Greg oiled his glove. He threw balls to his friends in the park. He let me wear his cap. He even pitched to Mom when it rained.

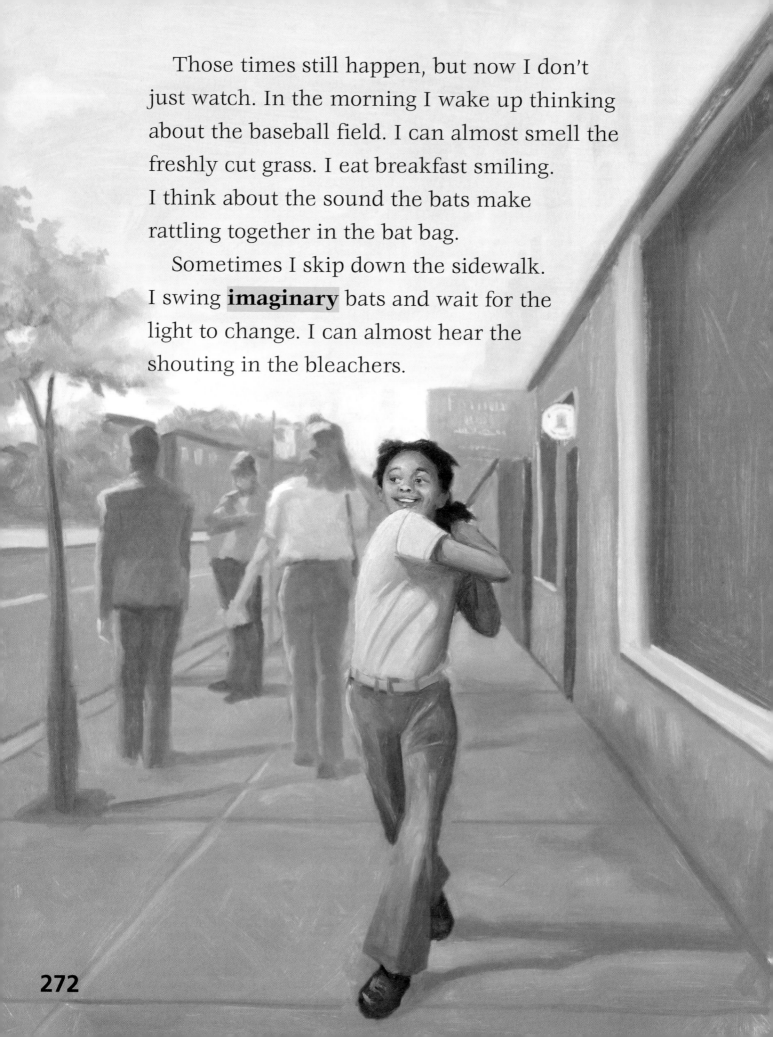

Those times still happen, but now I don't just watch. In the morning I wake up thinking about the baseball field. I can almost smell the freshly cut grass. I eat breakfast smiling. I think about the sound the bats make rattling together in the bat bag.

Sometimes I skip down the sidewalk. I swing **imaginary** bats and wait for the light to change. I can almost hear the shouting in the bleachers.

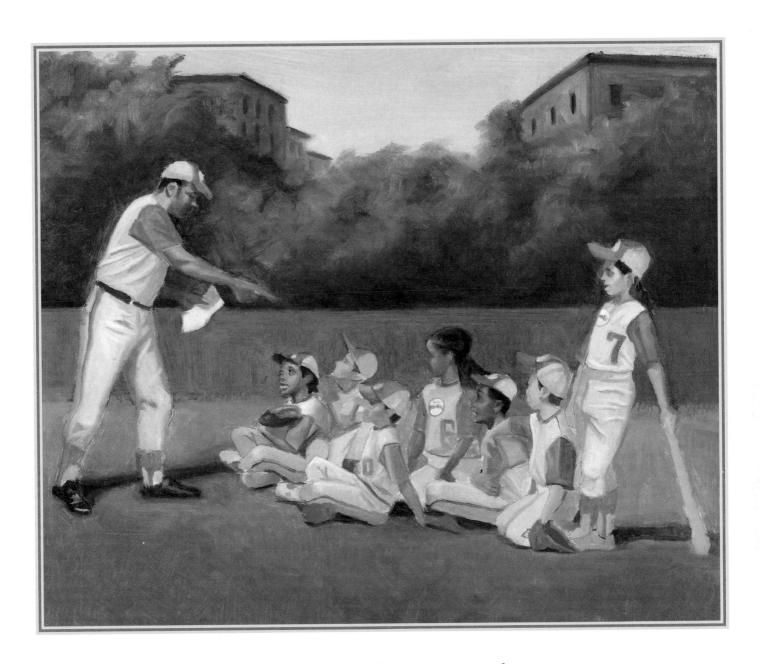

Jamal and I sit in the grass at the team
meetings. It's just like when we were little,
dreaming about baseball.

Now we are playing on the same team!

Make Inferences
Why do you think Emma likes
to play baseball so much?

We leave the field throwing baseballs up in the air. We count how many times in a row we can catch them.

We both laugh when we drop the balls. They roll down the sidewalk into the market, and we chase after them.

274

I stand in my **uniform** and look in the hall
mirror. I smile as I think of my brother in his
baseball uniform. I look at the picture of Mom
in her uniform. She was eight, like I am now.

I play on Rex's House of Fins and Fur baseball
team. Rex and his wife Sophie sponsor our team.
They own the pet store by the market. Rex and
Sophie bring snacks to all of our **practices**. And
they clap for everybody no matter what.

I like to think about baseball the way Rex
and Sophie do. They think you should try to
be the best, but most important to them is that
everybody gets to play.

A shortstop is what I want to be. I've wanted to be one ever since I saw my mom jump up real high to catch a ball. It was one summer night on the field. I saw her catch the hardest hit baseball I'd ever seen.

Shortstops are fast. A shortstop must reach to catch the high pops and dive to get the ground balls. A shortstop has to watch the whole infield.

The only problem is that Jamal wants to be shortstop, too.

I ask Jamal about the **tryouts** for our positions. "Who do you think will be shortstop?"

"I don't know," he says.

"I hope it's you," I say.

Jamal says, "I hope it's you, Emma."

But I don't say that the thing I want most in the world is to be the **starting** shortstop.

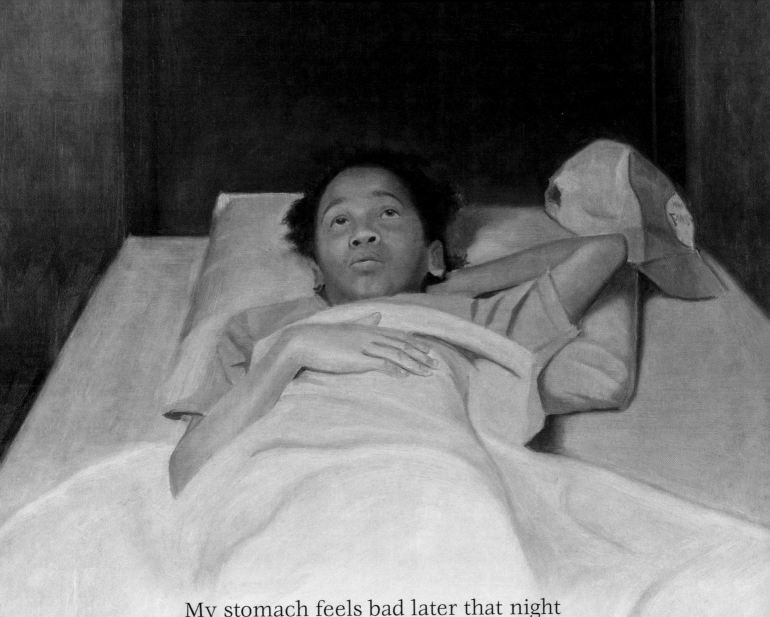

My stomach feels bad later that night when I wake up from a baseball dream. I'm happy in the dream but Jamal isn't. It's the first time I've ever felt bad about baseball.

For the next few days, the grass doesn't smell as good. The sound the bats make doesn't make me smile.

Make Inferences
Why do you think Emma feels bad when she wakes up from her dream?

279

Mom asks at dinner, "How's baseball practice going, Emma?"

I mash my beans with my potatoes and cover my chicken with it.

Mama smiles at my brother. "How's your practice going, Greg?"

He talks about his batting average. He wants to pitch more, too.

Greg says, "Emma, after dinner I can pitch a few to you."

I think how there's nothing better than when Greg pitches to me, but I'm still thinking about Jamal and me, too. Only one of us will get our wish.

The sun shines bright the next day at tryouts.
I stand beside Jamal and Nikki. The **coach** says
"good luck" to everybody.

I catch a base hit and throw to the catcher.
Jamal dives and catches a bounce to second.
Two outs.

I throw another batter out. Nikki jumps for a
line drive.

Our whole team is covered in dust. We are
all smiling at the end of the tryouts. There's
nothing like baseball.

The coach holds a meeting when we're done. I'll be playing second base. Jamal will play first. Nikki will play shortstop.

The coach is right. Nikki is better at shortstop than anybody. She can always jump the highest and make the best plays.

Jamal and I walk home together as the sun starts to set. We talk about how much fun the games will be as we toss the ball to each other.

This time of the day is the best part of all— because there's nothing like baseball.

On the Field with Angela and Eric

ANGELA JOHNSON

ERIC VELASQUEZ

"I love the idea of baseball," says **Angela Johnson**. "The lights, the smell, the fans." When she was young, Angela and her mother often went to watch her dad play baseball. "One of my earliest memories is crawling under the players' bench as my dad got up at bat. I can remember the sound the ball made hitting the bat."

Eric Velasquez says becoming an illustrator "was a natural choice for me. I have never thought of being anything else." He encourages young artists to "draw, draw, draw, paint, paint, paint, read, read, read."

Other books by Angela Johnson

LOG ON Find out more about Angela Johnson and Eric Velasquez at **www.macmillanmh.com**

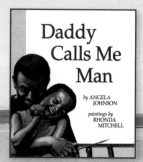

Daddy Calls Me Man
by ANGELA JOHNSON
paintings by RHONDA MITCHELL

JULIUS
STORY BY ANGELA JOHNSON
PICTURES BY DAV PILKEY

Author's Purpose
Angela Johnson wanted to write a story about baseball for readers to enjoy. Think about a sport or activity you like. Why do you like it? Write about your activity.

Comprehension Check

Retell the Story

Use the Retelling Cards to retell the story.

Retelling Cards

Think and Compare

1. Emma wants to be the **starting** shortstop for her team. Why is this a problem for her friendship with Jamal? **Ask Questions: Make Inferences**

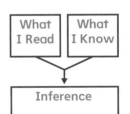

What I Read	What I Know

Inference

2. Reread pages 277–279. Why does Emma think that "The grass doesn't smell as good"? **Analyze**

3. Baseball is very important to Emma. What sport or activity do you do that you care a lot about? Explain why it is important to you. **Analyze**

4. Rex and Sophie think that everybody on the team should get to play. Why do you think that is important? **Synthesize**

5. Read "Brian Gets Fit on the Field" on pages 266–267. How are Brian and Emma alike? **Reading/Writing Across Texts**

Genre

Newspaper Articles give information and facts about current events.

Text Feature

Graphs show a relationship between numbers using bars or pictures.

Content Vocabulary

healthful

exercise

active

LINCOLN SCHOOL
NEWS

Students Stay Fit at School

by Ashley Marks

Students at Lincoln Elementary decided to make a difference this year. They came up with ideas to help the people in their town stay fit.

The children in kindergarten and first grade made lists of **healthful** foods that are good to eat. Some of the foods on their lists are apples, salad, and carrots. Juan Ramirez is in first grade. He says, "Eating right helps people feel better."

Students in the second and third grades have made lists of ways to **exercise** to help people stay fit. Some of the ideas on their lists are walking, riding bikes, and playing outdoor games.

Mai Wong is in second grade. She says, "Try to get moving for thirty minutes three or four days a week. You'll feel so much better if you're **active**!"

Students in second grade made a graph to show their favorite ways to stay fit.

How We Stay Fit

	0	5	10	15	20	25	30
baseball							
basketball							
bike riding							
running							
swimming							
walking							

This graph shows how students preferred to stay fit. At the left are the names of the activities. At the top you can see how many students enjoy that activity.

What have students in fourth and fifth grade done to help students stay fit? They hosted a Get Fit Fair. Students and their family members and friends from all around town came to learn more about getting fit and staying fit. What did people learn?

Oscar Jones has a daughter who goes to Lincoln. He and his daughter went to the Get Fit Fair. He says, "I learned that eating right and walking a lot will help me sleep better."

Don Fung's sister is a student at Lincoln. He says, "At the fair I found out that my thinking will be clearer if I eat right and get moving."

People tried all sorts of activities at the Get Fit Fair. Some danced. Some ran races. Some climbed stairs. Others played soccer and basketball.

Everyone had a great time at the Get Fit Fair. Lincoln School principal Maria Gomez said, "We plan to have this fair every year. We all learned a lot about healthful eating and how to be active."

Connect and Compare

1. What is the most popular way to stay fit among the students at the Lincoln School? **Graph**

2. Think about the story *There's Nothing Like Baseball*. If Emma and Jamal had attended the Get Fit Fair, what do you think they could have learned to get healthier? **Reading/Writing Across Texts**

 Health Activity

Research ways that you can get fit. Make a poster to share your ideas with others.

 Find out more about staying fit at **www.macmillanmh.com**

Write an Explanation

My Mom's Job
by May-Lin M.

After school I go to the community center to watch my mom work. She is a lifeguard. My mom's job is to keep people safe in the pool. Sometimes she blows her whistle to tell people to be careful. My mom also coaches my swim team. She helps us improve. The team swims faster now, and we know more strokes. My mom is a very smart and talented coach.

I used an 's after a word to show that someone has or owns something.

My mom is a good coach. I used precise words to tell why.

290

Your Turn

Write about something you like to do or someone you like to spend time with. Explain why. Use precise words that make your meaning clear. Use the Writer's Checklist to check your writing.

Writer's Checklist

☑ **Word Choice:** Did I use precise words that make my meaning clear?

☑ **Ideas:** Did I give good reasons for why I like to do something?

☑ **Conventions:** Did I add an apostrophe or an apostrophe and -s to make nouns possessive?

☑ **Sentence Fluency:** Did I vary the types of sentences in my writing?

Go Fly a Kite

by Lee Fischer

Go fly a kite! Have you ever heard that saying? Today there are different ways to fly kites. You could fly a kite in the sky, on the water, or even on the ground! The first kites were flown in China thousands of years ago. The kites were made of wood and paper. They had long, heavy tails. These kites needed a strong wind to fly.

Kites are fun to fly at the beach.

Go on ▶

Kite surfing is a new sport.

Today's kites are easier to fly. All they need is a light breeze. A beach or an open field is a great place to fly them.

If you are flying a kite at the beach, look around. You may see other kite flyers. Some of them fly on the water! They are called kite surfers.

Kite surfing is a new sport. It is a cross between kite flying and surfing. A kite surfer stands on a surfboard with a huge kite. The board has foot straps. The kite surfer controls the kite. The kite pulls the surfer across the water. Does kite surfing sound hard? It is!

Go on ▶ 293

Kite boarding is another new sport that uses kites. Kite boarders use kites with skateboards. Some may use roller skates instead. Kite boarders use parking lots, fields, and other open spaces. With wheels beneath their feet, they can really speed ahead!

Kite boarders wear gear for safety.

Go on ▶

Tip

Connect the clues.

Directions:
Answer the questions.

1. **Why are today's kites easier to fly?**

    A   Kids start when they are younger.

    B   They run on batteries.

    C   The materials are lighter.

    D   Winds are stronger now.

2. **Why is kite boarding an unusual sport?**

    A   It is very safe.

    B   It puts two different sports together.

    C   You can only do it in the summer.

    D   It can be done only at the beach.

3. **Tell why kite surfing is hard to do.**

Writing Prompt

Write an explanation of how to play your favorite sport. Include details and number each step.

Telling Stories

Talk About It

What makes a great story? Why do you think people like to tell stories?

LOG ON Find out more about telling stories at **www.macmillanmh.com**

The Story of the  Giant Carrot

by Rosa Manuel

One day Farmer Smith planted carrot seeds. The next morning he looked outside and **gasped**. He took a gulp of air because he was so surprised. A giant leaf was growing in the garden. He knew what would be **attached**. Giant leaves are joined to giant carrots!

298

Farmer Smith ran outside **frantically**. He was very, very excited. He jumped up and grabbed the leaf. It was so high, he **swung** from it! His body waved from side to side. Once his feet were back on the ground, he pulled on the leaf. The giant carrot would not come out.

First, he called to his family for help. The family pulled, but the carrot was too big. Then he asked his neighbors to help. They pulled so hard that they had to stop to **breathe**. It was hard for them to get enough air. Finally, he called to the dog and cow for help. They all pulled, and at last the carrot popped out!

The Smith family fed the whole town with the **delicious** carrot. Everyone said it was the best-tasting carrot they had ever eaten!

Reread for **Comprehension**

Reread
Cause and Effect
Rereading a story can help you understand the cause and effects of events in the story. A cause is why something happens. An effect is what happens. Use the chart as you reread the story.

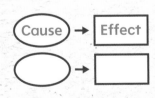

Comprehension

Genre

A **Folk Tale** is usually a made-up story that takes place long ago.

Reread

Cause and Effect

As you read, use your Cause and Effect Chart.

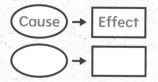

Read to Find Out

What causes the body parts to try to work together?

Head, Body, Legs

A Story from Liberia

retold by
Won-Ldy Paye & Margaret H. Lippert
illustrated by Julie Paschkis

Award Winning Author

Long ago, Head was all by himself.

He had no legs, no arms, no body. He rolled everywhere. All he could eat were things on the ground that he could reach with his tongue.

At night he rolled under a cherry tree. He fell asleep and dreamed of sweet cherries.

One morning Head woke up and thought, "I'm tired of grass and mushrooms. I wish I could reach those cherries."

He rolled himself up a little hill. "Maybe if I get a good head start I can hit the trunk hard enough to knock some cherries off," he thought. He shoved with his ears and began to roll down the hill. "Here I go!" he shouted.

Faster and faster he rolled.

CRASH!

"OWWWW!" he cried.

"Who's there?" someone asked.

Head looked up.
Above him **swung**
two Arms he had
never seen before.

"Look down here,"
Head said, "and
you'll see."

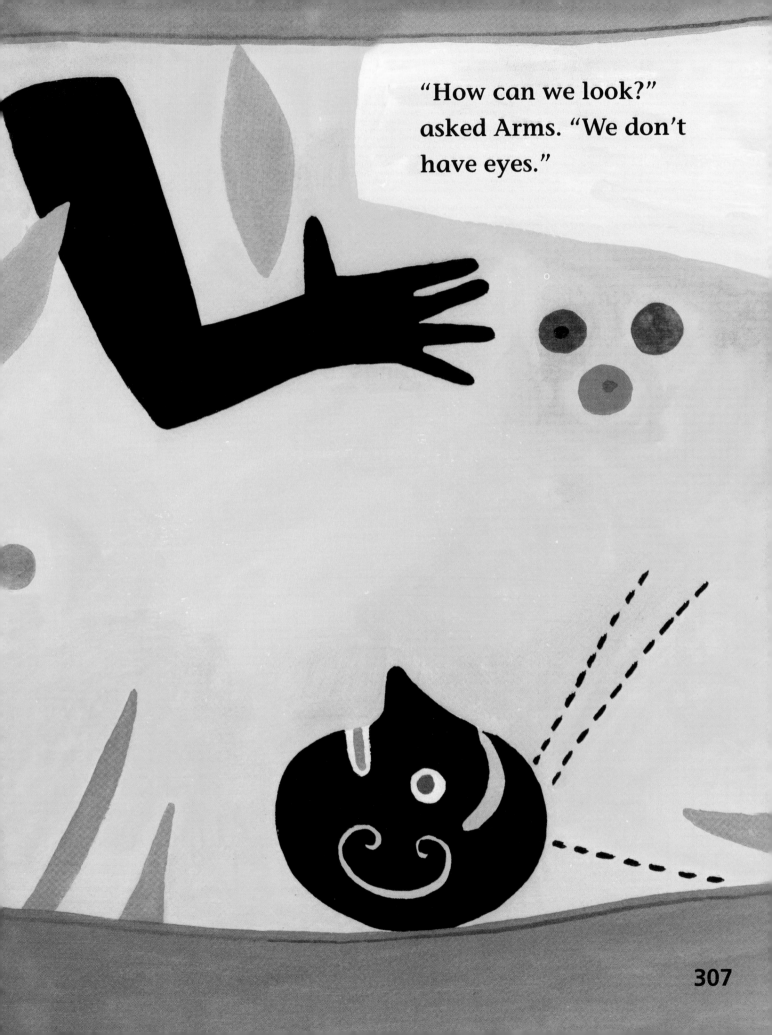

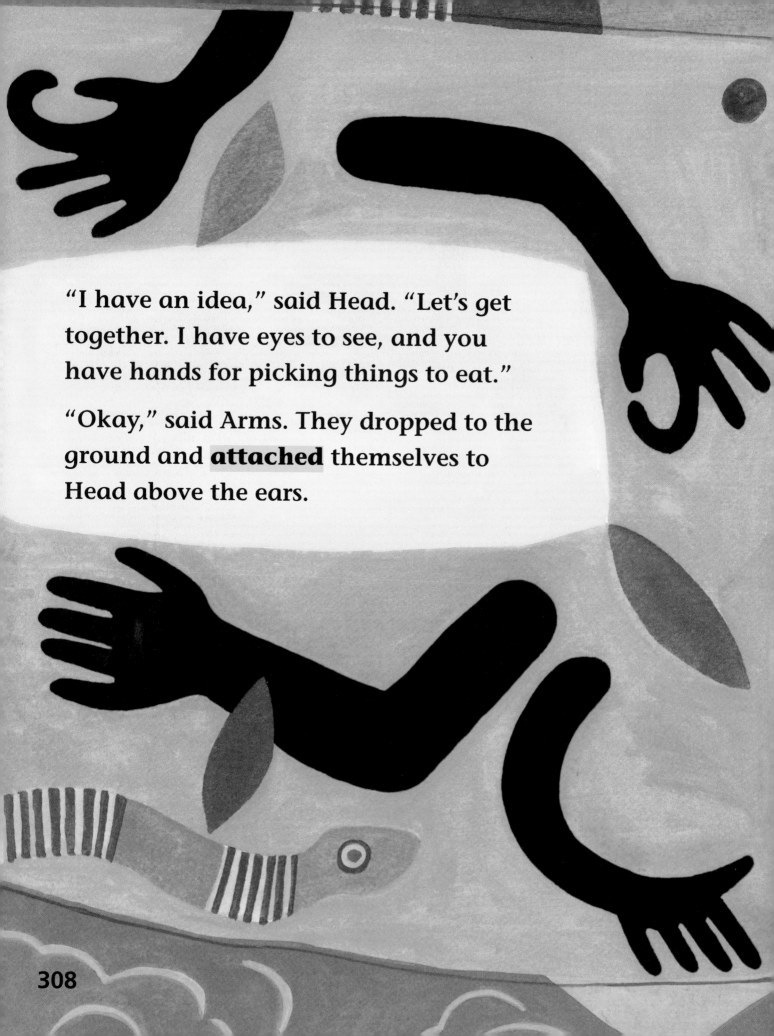

"I have an idea," said Head. "Let's get together. I have eyes to see, and you have hands for picking things to eat."

"Okay," said Arms. They dropped to the ground and **attached** themselves to Head above the ears.

"This," said Head, "is perfect."

STRATEGY
SKILL
Cause and Effect
What will Head and Arms be able to do now that they are attached?

Hands picked cherries, and Head ate every single one.

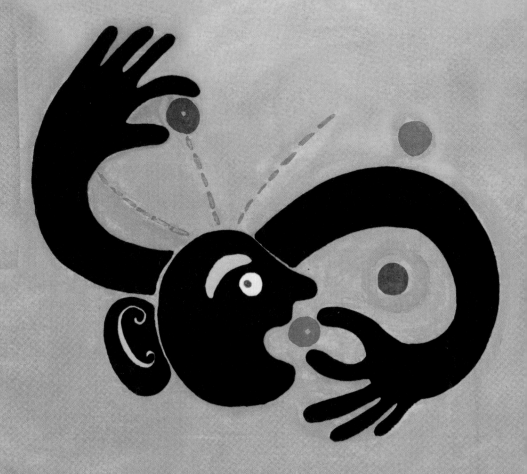

"It's time for a nap," said Head, yawning. Soon he was fast asleep.

While Head slept, Body bounced along and landed on top of him.

"Help!" **gasped** Head. "I can't **breathe**!" Arms pushed Body off.

"Hey," said Body. "Stop pushing me. Who are you?"

"It's us, Head and Arms," said Head. "You almost squashed us. Watch where you're going!"

"How can I?" asked Body. "I can't see."

"Why don't you join us?" said Head. "I see some ripe mangoes across the river. If you help us swim over there, I'll help you see where you're going."

"Okay," said Body. So Head attached himself to Body at the belly button.

"This," said Head,
"is perfect."

They bounced down the bank into the river.

"Pull right . . . pull left," Head shouted to Arms, who paddled **frantically** against the current.

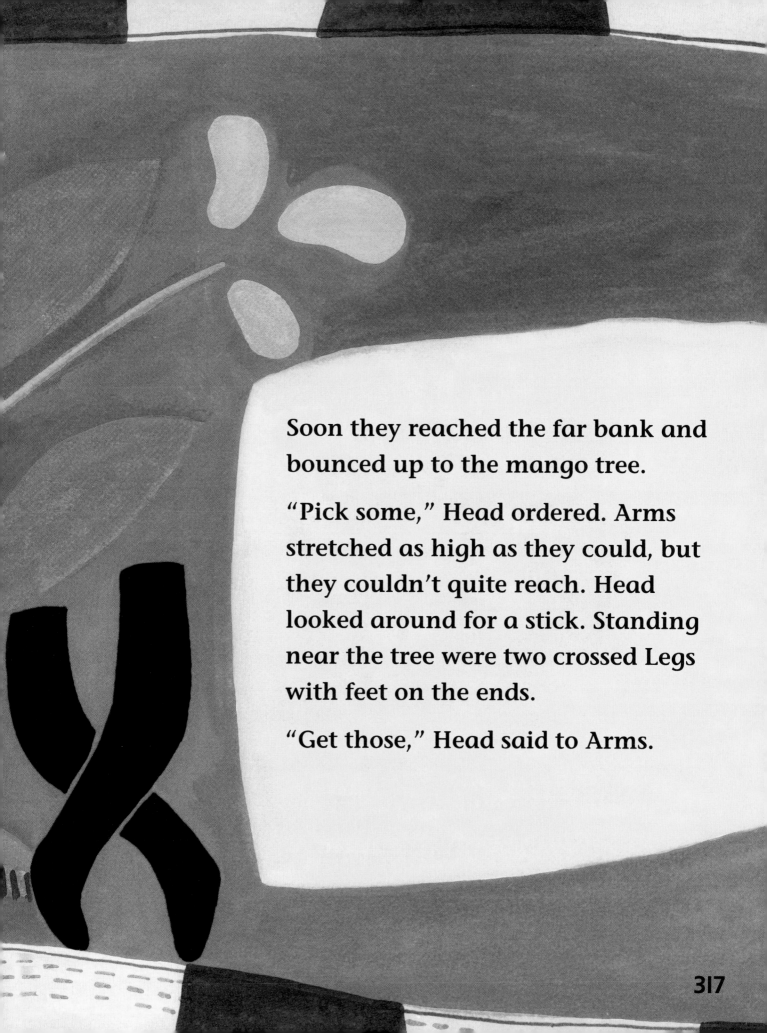

Soon they reached the far bank and bounced up to the mango tree.

"Pick some," Head ordered. Arms stretched as high as they could, but they couldn't quite reach. Head looked around for a stick. Standing near the tree were two crossed Legs with feet on the ends.

"Get those," Head said to Arms.

Arms grabbed them.
"Let us go!" shouted Legs.

"Who are you?" asked Head.

"We're Legs. We were
walking but we bumped
into this tree."

"Join us," said Head. "I have eyes. I can show you where to go, and you can help us reach those mangoes."

"Okay," said Legs. So Legs attached themselves to the hands.

Cause and Effect
How can Legs help the others reach the mangoes?

320

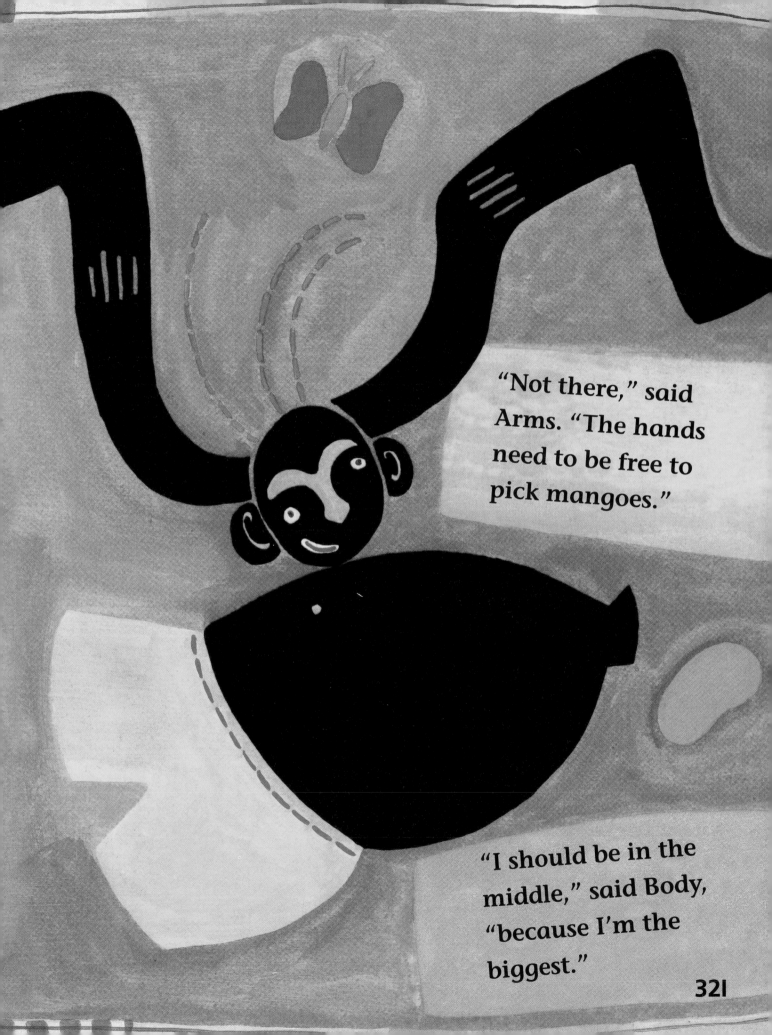

"Not there," said Arms. "The hands need to be free to pick mangoes."

"I should be in the middle," said Body, "because I'm the biggest."

"That's right," said Head. "You should be at the bottom, Legs. I'll swing around on top of Body so I can see everything. And Arms, you move to the shoulders."

Everyone slid into place. Legs stood on tiptoe. Body straightened out. Arms stretched up and the hands picked a mango. Head took a bite.

"Mmm, **delicious**," Head said.
"Now THIS is perfect!"

Telling Stories with the Authors and Illustrator

Won-Ldy Paye came to this country from Liberia, which is in Africa. He is a storyteller as well as a writer. To write *Head, Body, Legs*, Won-Ldy worked with children's writer **Margaret Lippert**. Margaret travels all over the world learning folk stories. She shares her stories by writing children's books.

Artist **Julie Paschkis** is also a storyteller. She says she tells stories through her art. Julie has illustrated many children's books.

Another book by Won-Ldy Paye, Margaret Lippert, and Julie Paschkis

 LOG ON Find out more about Won-Ldy Paye and Julie Paschkis at **www.macmillanmh.com**

Author's Purpose
Won-Ldy Paye wrote this story about working together for readers to enjoy. Think about a time you worked with others. Write about it.

Comprehension Check

Retell the Story

Use the Retelling Cards to retell the story.

Retelling Cards

Think and Compare

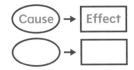

1. What happens when all the body parts join together? **Reread: Cause and Effect**

2. Reread pages 320–323. Why do the body parts change places several times? **Analyze**

3. Do you think Head did the right thing when he and Arms **attached** themselves to each other? Explain. **Evaluate**

4. What did you learn from this tale? How is it important in real life? **Apply**

5. How is *Head, Body, Legs* like "The Story of the Giant Carrot" on pages 298–299? **Reading/ Writing Across Texts**

Favorites \ History \ Search \ Scrapbook

Language Arts

Genre
An **Internet Article** gives information about a topic and is found on the World Wide Web.

Text Feature
The **Drop-Down Menu** in an Internet article has links to related information on the Web site.

Content Vocabulary
orally

tradition

festivals

Telling Tales

What is your favorite story? It doesn't have to be one from a book. Some of the best stories are ones that family and friends tell about things that have happened to them. These stories are passed on **orally** from person to person.

Storytelling is a **tradition** that has been around for a very long time. Long ago, storytelling was a way of spreading news of important events.

Today, storytelling **festivals** are held around the world. These celebrations are a way for people to pass on their stories.

Storytelling Links

For more information about storytelling check out:

- Guide to U.S. Storytellers
- Storytelling Festivals Around the World
- Index of Famous Historical Storytellers

Connect and Compare

1. What other information about storytelling can you link to in this article? **Drop-Down Menu**

2. Think about this article and *Head, Body, Legs: A Story from Liberia.* Do you think this story was once part of an oral tradition? Explain why or why not. **Reading/Writing Across Texts**

 Language Arts Activity

Research folk tales online. Choose a folk tale you like and tell it to your class.

 Find more about oral traditions at **www.macmillanmh.com**

Writer's Craft

Unimportant Details
One way to make your writing easy to understand is to take out any unimportant details. Also make sure the pictures match the text.

Make a Poster

Reasons to Read

Reading can be a lot of fun. Here are some reasons why I think people should read a lot.

1. Reading is a good way to relax.

2. Books describe amazing places around the world.

3. Reading a little bit every day makes it easier to finish long books.

4. There's always something new to learn about in a book.

I took out an unimportant detail about my favorite book.

The picture I drew matches my writing.

Your Turn

Make your own poster that tells why something is important to you. Use words and pictures that will make your message clear. Take out unimportant details. Then use the Writer's Checklist to check your writing.

Writer's Checklist

☑ **Ideas:** Did I take out unimportant details? Do my pictures match my words?

☑ **Word Choice:** Did I choose strong words to get my message across?

☑ **Conventions:** Did I use action verbs?

☑ **Sentence Fluency:** Did I write sentences that are short and to the point?

Safety First

Talk About It

What do you do to stay safe when you play outside? Why is wearing safety gear important?

LOG ON Find out more about safety at **www.macmillanmh.com**

SAFETY AT SCHOOL

by Brian Sullivan

"We need to talk about the school rules," our teacher, Mr. Wall, said. It was the second day of school. "What do you do when I turn out the lights?"

"Pay **attention** and listen carefully to you," said Pete.

"Good," said Mr. Wall. "What about lining up?"

"Find your line **buddy** and stand in line at the door," said Rosa.

334

"Right!" said Mr. Wall. "Remember, your line buddy is the friend you line up with. What is another rule, Julia?"

"No running in the halls," Julia said. "No one wants to fall or slip and have an **accident**."

"Good **tip**," said Mr. Wall. "That's helpful information to keep in mind. Also, why should we stay together in the halls?"

"This school is **enormous**. It's so huge it would be easy to get lost," said Liam.

"I know you all will follow the rules," said Mr. Wall. "When everyone **obeys** them, we stay safe."

Reread for **Comprehension**

Read Ahead
Illustrations

Reading ahead in a story can include looking at the illustrations. Looking at illustrations can help you understand what you read. Reread the story and use the chart to understand what the illustrations tell you about the story.

Illustration	What I Learn From the Picture

Comprehension

Genre
Fiction is a story with made-up characters and events.

Read Ahead
Use Illustrations
As you read and look at the pictures, use the Illustrations Chart.

Illustration	What I Learn From the Picture

Read to Find Out
How do the illustrations help make the story funny?

WASH YOUR HANDS AFTER YOU USE THE TOILET.

NEVER PLAY WITH MATCHES.

NEVER PUT ANYTHING IN YOUR EAR.

OBEY ALL TRAFFIC SIGNS.

NEVER BOTHER A BIG DOG WHILE IT'S EATING.

NEVER SIT TOO CLOSE TO THE TELEVISION.

NEVER EAT MAYONNAISE THAT'S BEEN SITTING IN THE SUN.

336

OFFICER BUCKLE AND GLORIA

written and illustrated
by Peggy Rathmann

Officer Buckle knew more safety **tips** than anyone else in Napville.

Every time he thought of a new one, he thumbtacked it to his bulletin board.

Safety Tip #77
NEVER stand on a SWIVEL CHAIR.

Officer Buckle shared his safety tips with the students at Napville School.

Nobody ever listened.

Sometimes, there was snoring.

Afterward, it was business as usual.

Mrs. Toppel, the principal, took down the welcome banner.

"NEVER stand on a SWIVEL CHAIR," said Officer Buckle, but Mrs. Toppel didn't hear him.

Then one day, Napville's police department bought a police dog named Gloria.

When it was time for Officer Buckle to give the safety speech at the school, Gloria went along.

"Children, this is Gloria," announced Officer Buckle. "Gloria **obeys** my commands. Gloria, SIT!" And Gloria sat.

Officer Buckle gave Safety Tip Number One:

"KEEP your SHOELACES tied!"

The children sat up and stared.
Officer Buckle checked to see if Gloria
was sitting at **attention**. She was.

"Safety Tip Number Two," said
Officer Buckle.

**"ALWAYS wipe up spills BEFORE
someone SLIPS AND FALLS!"**

The children's eyes popped.
Officer Buckle checked on
Gloria again.
"Good dog," he said.

Officer Buckle thought of a safety tip he had discovered that morning.

"NEVER leave a THUMBTACK where you might SIT on it!"

The audience roared.

 Use Illustrations
How does Gloria make Officer Buckle's speeches more interesting?

Officer Buckle grinned. He said the rest of the tips with *plenty* of expression.

The children clapped their hands and cheered. Some of them laughed until they cried.

Officer Buckle was surprised. He had never noticed how funny safety tips could be.

After *this* safety speech, there wasn't a single **accident**.

The next day, an **enormous** envelope
arrived at the police station. It was stuffed
with thank-you letters from the students at
Napville School.

Every letter had a drawing
of Gloria on it.

Officer Buckle thought
the drawings showed a lot
of imagination.

His favorite letter was written on a star-shaped piece of paper. It said:

You and Gloria make a good team.

Your friend,
Claire

P.S. I always wear a crash helmet. (Safety Tip #7)

Officer Buckle was thumbtacking Claire's letter to his bulletin board when the phones started ringing. Grade schools, high schools, and day-care centers were calling about the safety speech.

"Officer Buckle," they said, "our students want to hear your safety tips! And please, bring along that police dog."

Officer Buckle told his safety tips to
313 schools. Everywhere he and Gloria went,
children sat up and listened.

After every speech, Officer Buckle took
Gloria out for ice cream.
Officer Buckle loved having a **buddy**.

Then one day, a television news team videotaped Officer Buckle in the state college auditorium.

When he finished Safety Tip Number Ninety-nine,

DO NOT GO SWIMMING DURING ELECTRICAL STORMS!,

the students jumped to their feet and applauded.

"Bravo! Bravo!" they cheered.
Officer Buckle bowed again and again.

That night, Officer Buckle watched
himself on the 10 o'clock news.

 Use Illustrations
What does Officer Buckle find out
about his safety speeches? Use the
illustrations to explain your answer.

The next day, the principal of Napville School telephoned the police station.

"Good morning, Officer Buckle! It's time for our safety speech!"

Officer Buckle frowned.

"I'm not giving any more speeches! Nobody looks at me, anyway!"

"Oh," said Mrs. Toppel. "Well! How about Gloria? Could she come?"

Someone else from the police station gave
Gloria a ride to the school.

Gloria sat onstage looking lonely. Then she
fell asleep. So did the audience.

After Gloria left, Napville School had its
biggest accident ever....

It started with a puddle of banana pudding....

SPLAT!
SPLATTER!
SPLOOSH!

Everyone slid smack into Mrs. Toppel,
who screamed and
let go of her hammer.

The next morning, a pile of letters arrived at the police station.

Every letter had a drawing of the accident.

Officer Buckle was shocked.

At the bottom of the pile was a note written on a paper star.

Officer Buckle smiled.

The note said:

Gloria missed you yesterday!
Your friend,
Claire

P.S. Don't worry,
I was wearing
my helmet!
(Safety Tip #7)

Gloria gave Officer Buckle a big kiss on the nose. Officer Buckle gave Gloria a nice pat on the back. Then, Officer Buckle thought of his best safety tip yet...

Safety Tip #101

"ALWAYS STICK WITH YOUR BUDDY!"

A GOOD LAUGH WITH PEGGY RATHMANN

Peggy Rathmann got the idea for *Officer Buckle and Gloria* from a videotape. The tape shows Peggy's mother talking. In the background, the dog licks the eggs that were set out for breakfast.

The next part of the tape, Peggy says, "shows the whole family at the breakfast table, complimenting my mother on the delicious eggs." Of course, no one knew what the dog had done! "The first time we watched that tape we were so shocked, we couldn't stop laughing," Peggy says.

Other books written by Peggy Rathmann

 Find out more about Peggy Rathmann at **www.macmillanmh.com**

Author's Purpose

Peggy Rathmann wanted to write a funny story about a dog that helps its owner. Write about something kind you did. Did anyone find out?

Comprehension Check

Retell the Story

Use the Retelling Cards to retell the story.

Retelling Cards

Think and Compare

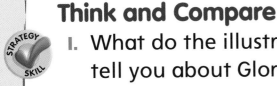

1. What do the illustrations tell you about Gloria's personality? **Read Ahead: Use Illustrations**

Illustration	What I Learn From the Picture

2. Reread pages 341–343. Why does no one listen to Officer Buckle's safety **tips**? Use the text and the illustrations to explain. **Apply**

3. Would you like to have a dog like Gloria? Why or why not? **Evaluate**

4. Why is "Always stick with your buddy" an important tip? **Synthesize**

5. How are the safety tips in "Safety at School" on pages 334–335 different from Officer Buckle's tips? **Reading/Writing Across Texts**

Fire Safety

Firefighters want everyone to be safe. They teach families how to avoid fire **hazards**, which are dangerous items or situations. You can help prevent fires by following fire safety rules. You can also stay safe by knowing what to do if a fire starts nearby.

How to Stay Safe from Fire

- Never play with matches or lighters.

- Do not touch lit candles.

- Do not cook unless an adult is with you.

- Be careful around irons, stoves, fireplaces, and grills.

- Never touch electric cords, plugs, or outlets.

Stop! Drop! Roll!

If your clothes catch fire, do these three things right away.

1

2

3

Stop! Running and walking can make fire worse.

Drop! Get down on the ground. Cover your face and eyes.

Roll! Roll over and over until the flames are out.

363

Make a Plan!

You and your family can learn how to stay safe if there is a fire in your home. Make a floor plan of your home. Mark the best ways to get out of the house. Make sure your plan has more than one **route** in case one path gets blocked. Pick a safe place to meet outside. Have fire drills to practice your plan. Practicing will help you stay **calm** and find a safe path to the outside.

Fire Safety Floor Plan

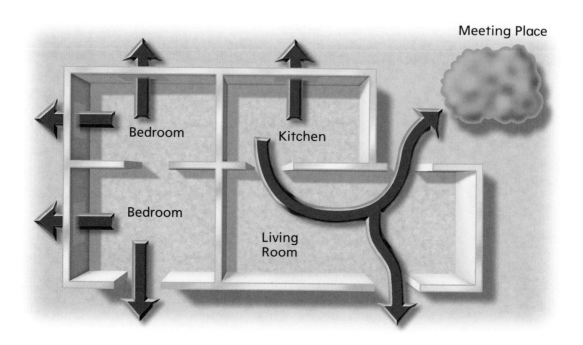

This floor plan shows several ways to get out of a home in case a fire starts.

After you are safely out of the house, call 9-1-1 for help. Wait for the firefighters to arrive. Never go back into the house for anything!

Connect and Compare

1. What two escape routes from each bedroom does the floor plan show? **Floor Plan**

2. Think about this article and *Officer Buckle and Gloria.* What are some other safety tips that firefighters might try to teach to students and families? **Reading/Writing Across Texts**

 Health Activity

Draw a floor plan of your home. Show at least two escape routes and your outside meeting place. Give a copy to your family.

LOG ON Find out more about fire safety at **www.macmillanmh.com**

Write a Speech

Wear Your Bike Helmet
by Jay F.

My speech begins with a strong opening that states my message.

I love riding my bike really fast, but it's important to be safe. Wearing a bike helmet every time you ride is very important. Just last week I fell off my bike. But when my head hit the street, my helmet protected it. What would have happened if I hadn't worn my helmet? I hate to think about it!

I used present-tense verbs to help get my message across.

My helmet keeps me from getting really hurt. So be safe! Wear your bike helmet each time you ride!

Your Turn

Write your own speech about safety.
Begin with a strong opening sentence.
Tell why safety is so important. Try to
get your listeners to agree with you.
Then use the Writer's Checklist to
check your writing.

Writer's Checklist

☑ **Ideas:** Did I use a **strong opening** that makes my message strong and clear?

☑ **Voice:** Will my speech make others agree with my message?

☑ **Conventions:** Did I use present-tense verbs correctly?

☑ **Sentence Fluency:** Did I use different kinds of sentences to make my speech more interesting?

How do we learn about animals that lived long, long ago?

LOG ON Find out more about dinosaurs at **www.macmillanmh.com**

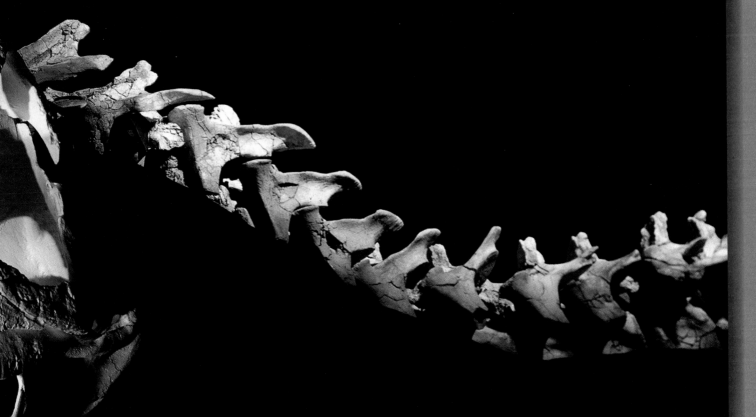

CREATURES OLD...

AND OLDER

TIME FOR KIDS

Coelacanth

Coelacanth

Vocabulary

ancient
hopeful
unable
confirm
valid

AFRICA

N
W E
S

Madagascar

Coelacanth
Fish Location

A VERY OLD FISH

The coelacanth (SEE-luh-kanth) is an **ancient** fish. It lived about 360 million years ago. People first learned about the coelacanth by studying its fossils. Fossils are the shapes or remains left behind by something that lived a long time ago.

People believed that the coelacanths died millions of years ago. But in 1938, a fisherman caught a coelacanth near Madagascar. Since then more have been caught. Now scientists are **hopeful** they can protect coelacanths. They believe they can help because the scientists have learned more about the fish. Coelacanths are **unable** to live in the warm water near the top of the ocean. They can only live deep underwater.

370

Scientists made a model of the lizard that lived millions of years ago.

This fossil is the head of the ancient lizard.

BOY FINDS FOSSILS!

In 1999, twelve-year-old Miguel Avelas amazed scientists all over the world. Miguel discovered hundreds of fossils in Patagonia, in the southern part of South America. Miguel led a team of scientists to the fossils. The scientists guessed the fossils were from a lizard.

The scientists studied the fossils and were able to **confirm** that their idea was correct. The fossils gave them **valid** information that this lizard had lived more than 120 million years ago. Now they had proof that it had lived in Patagonia. Miguel's discovery gave the scientists important new information.

LOG ON Find out more about fossils at www.macmillanmh.com

Meet the Super Croc

Did a crocodile the size of a school bus once live on Earth?

What kind of animal was it? Its body was about 40 feet long. That's about the size of a school bus. Its jaws were about 5 feet long. That's about as long as some people are tall! It had about 100 teeth.

Name: *Sarcosuchus imperator* ("Super Croc")
Length: Up to 50 feet
Weight: About 17,500 pounds
Lived: About 110 million years ago

This powerful creature hid in the water, waiting for an animal to come to the river for a drink. Any animal that was grabbed by those teeth would be **unable** to get away.

Don't worry! This toothy giant is no longer alive today. It lived about 110 million years ago, when dinosaurs roamed the Earth. That's about 105 million years before human beings were around.

This drawing shows what scientists think "Super Croc" looked like.

Name: Australian crocodile
Length: Up to 23 feet
Weight: About 2,000 pounds
Lives: Alive today

Name: American alligator
Length: Up to 20 feet
Weight: About 1,300 pounds
Lives: Alive today

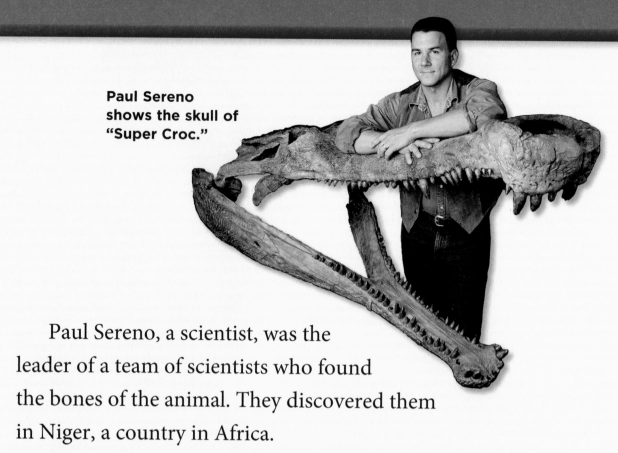

Paul Sereno, a scientist, was the leader of a team of scientists who found the bones of the animal. They discovered them in Niger, a country in Africa.

Sereno and his team were **hopeful** the bones belonged to a kind of giant crocodile from the time of the dinosaurs. But they weren't sure. The whole team needed to study the bones before they could **confirm** their theory. They compared the bones to the bodies of crocodiles living today. If the bones were similar, the theory would be **valid**.

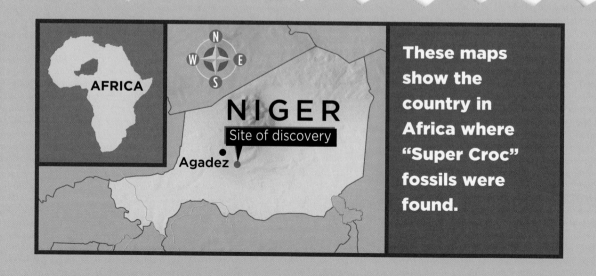

AFRICA

N
W E
S

NIGER
Site of discovery
Agadez

These maps show the country in Africa where "Super Croc" fossils were found.

The shape of the head and skull bones gave Sereno and his team the proof they were looking for. The **ancient** bones belonged to a "Super Croc" that lived at the same time the dinosaurs lived on Earth.

Sereno made copies of the bones to keep in the United States. The original bones were sent back to the country of Niger. If you want to see the real "Super Croc," the bones are on display in a museum there.

A young boy checks out the model of "Super Croc."

Think and Compare

1. How would you summarize this article?

2. How did Paul Sereno prove his theory?

3. If you were a scientist like Paul Sereno, what would you want to study?

4. Compare the creature described in "Boy Finds Fossils!" with "Super Croc." How are they the same? How are they different?

Some Strange Teeth

 **Test Strategy**

Think and Search
Read on to find the answer. Look for information in more than one place.

Scientist David Krause digs for fossils on Madagascar.

Dinosaur fossil hunters were digging on Madagascar. It is an island off the coast of Africa. The team found something that looked like the lower jaw of an animal. It had strange sharp teeth. Was it a dinosaur bone?

"We thought it could be a crocodile or a flying reptile," the team leader said. Scientists studied the hook-shaped teeth. The team discovered that this animal lived 70 million years ago and ate fish and insects. For a dinosaur, it wasn't very big.

Madagascar is a good place for finding dinosaur bones. The oldest dinosaur bones ever found were dug up there. Scientists will keep looking. One scientist said, "We still don't know everything about dinosaurs."

Go On ▶

Directions: Answer the questions.

1. What did fossil hunters find?

   A   the jaw of an old fish

   B   the teeth of a crocodile

   C   the bones of a flying reptile

   D   the jaw of a small dinosaur

2. What was unusual about the jaw bone?

   A   There was no upper jaw.

   B   It was very big.

   C   The teeth could not chew food.

   D   The sharp teeth looked like hooks.

Tip
Look for
information.

3. How do these scientists feel about their work?

   A   It is a waste of time to dig for bones.

   B   They can work only in Madagascar.

   C   There is nothing left to find.

   D   There is still more to learn.

4. Summarize the article about the new dinosaur found on Madagascar.

5. Why would someone want to hunt for dinosaur bones? Is this something that you would be interested in doing? Use details from the article to support your answer.

Write to a Prompt

The selections describe different ways people can work together. Write about a time when teamwork helped you do a job. Your story should have at least three paragraphs.

My story has a beginning, a middle, and an ending.

Finding Peanut

One day I could not find my cat Peanut. He stays in the house most of the time, but sometimes he goes into the yard.

Peanut was not in the house. He was not in the yard. I looked all over and called his name. Soon my friend Tracy next door heard me. She said, "Can I help?"

"You go that way," I said. "I'll go this way." I did not see Peanut anywhere.

After a while Tracy came around the corner carrying Peanut! "He was in a tree," Tracy said. "A big dog was barking at him."

I thanked Tracy. I might not have found Peanut without her help.

Your Writing Prompt

Some jobs can be done by one person. But for many jobs, like digging up dinosaur bones, teamwork is best. Write about a time you worked with a partner or a team. Tell what you did together. Make sure your story has a beginning, a middle, and an ending. Your story should be two or three paragraphs long.

Writer's Checklist

- ✔ Think about your purpose for writing.

- ✔ Use details to support your story.

- ✔ Be sure your story has a beginning, a middle, and an ending.

- ✔ Use your best spelling, grammar, and punctuation.

Curtain Up!

Vocabulary

students
perform
effort
remember
mood
proud

Thesaurus

Antonyms are words that have opposite meanings.

Remember and *forget* are antonyms.

A Little Symphony

by Lani Perlin

The Fresno Little Symphony is a group of young people who play music. The **students** are children who study and learn music together. They have shows where they play their music for others. Sometimes they **perform** in front of many people.

382

It takes a lot of **effort** to be part of a symphony. The students work hard to do their best. They practice once a week. This helps them **remember** how to play the songs. They do not want to forget the music.

The students can play many different songs. Each song has its own **mood**. The mood is the feeling that people get when they listen to the music.

One thing is always the same, though. People leave the shows feeling glad. The people who live in Fresno are **proud** of the symphony. Many are happy to say it is the best little symphony in California!

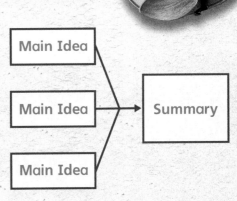

Reread for **Comprehension**

Visualize
Summarize

Visualizing, or forming pictures in your mind, can help you summarize what you are reading. When you summarize an article, you tell the most important parts or main ideas. Reread the article and use the chart to summarize.

Main Idea	
Main Idea	Summary
Main Idea	

383

Genre

Nonfiction gives information and facts about a topic.

Visualize

Summarize

As you read, use the Summarize Chart.

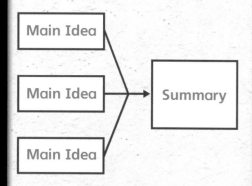

Main Idea

Main Idea → Summary

Main Idea

Read to Find Out

Who are the Alvin Ailey kids and what do they do?

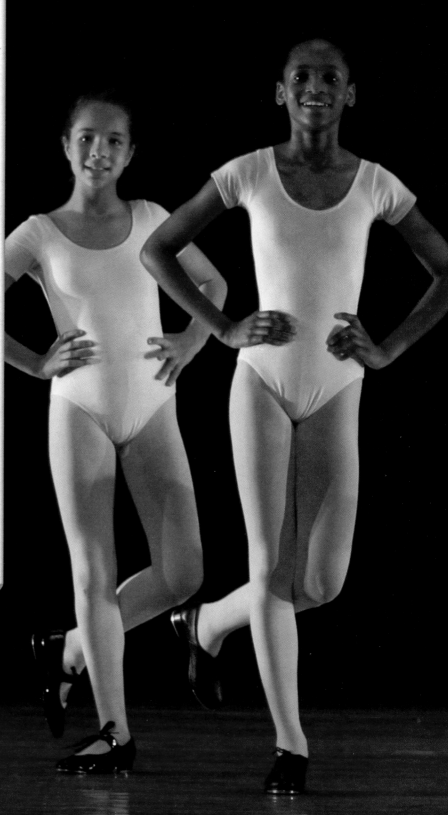

The Alvin Ailey Kids
Dancing
As a Team

by
Sharon Dennis Wyeth

Alvin Ailey Kids

At The Alvin Ailey School in New York City, kids study dance. They take dance classes after school. They take classes on Saturday. Hundreds of **students** dance at the school.

Each spring the students at Ailey **perform** in front of an audience. The dancers show what they have learned during the year.

Dancing is hard work. The steps have to be done just right. That takes a lot of practice. It's also a team **effort**.

The teachers help the students learn the steps. They try to make the classes fun. The musicians also do their part. The kids have a great time while they are learning.

Summarize
Who helps the students at Ailey learn to dance? How do they help?

Getting Ready in the Spring

J asper and Whitney attended the Ailey school in the spring of 2004. Jasper was nine years old. Whitney was ten. Jasper started to dance when he was four. When Whitney was very young, she went with her family to a ballet.

"I knew then that I wanted to dance myself," said Whitney. "Dance helps me to express myself."

Jasper, Whitney, and the other Ailey students were excited in May. Their performance was coming up. They had two more weeks to practice. Then they would perform in a real theater.

They would show their parents and friends what they had learned. First, they had more work to do to get ready for the show.

389

Dance Classes

The girls in Whitney's ballet class practiced their steps. Their teacher, Melanie, helped them. She wanted them to do their best.

"Arms open, girls!" Melanie told them.

Teamwork was a big part of the dance. Everyone had to do the steps at exactly the same time. "You have to dance in two ways on stage, by yourself and with a group," said Melanie.

The same girls also took tap class. The **mood** is different in tap. The music is jazzy! The shoes are noisy!

The girls tapped, stomped, and marched to the music. The dance they were going to perform was long. The students did not always **remember** all the steps. It was also hard to stay together.

"We have some more work to do," said their teacher, Vic. "From the top! 5, 6, 7, 8 smile!" Vic worked for a long time with the girls.

Jasper's favorite class was capoeira. It is a type of circle dance. To warm up, the boys stretched. They did kicks and jumps.

To do the dance, two boys went into the middle of a circle. They kicked and moved fast. All the boys took turns. They moved in and out of the circle. The boys also sang and clapped to the music.

Jasper talked excitedly about the class. "I love to dance," he said. "The thing I like best about dance is the beat!"

Capoeira

(kah-poo-air-ah) is a dance from Brazil. Everyone forms a circle for the roda, or circle dance. They sing and clap. The dancers all have bare feet. Musicians play different instruments.

Dress Rehearsal

The day of the dress rehearsal arrived. A dress rehearsal is a final practice before the performance. It is held where the show will take place.

The students went to the theater. They thought the stage was huge. The stage manager showed them how to enter and exit the stage properly.

There were new things to get used to at the dress rehearsal. Moving on the big stage felt different. The lights were also something new.

"Watch your spacing!" said Christine, a ballet teacher. "Remember you are dancing together." The students practiced their dances one last time. The next time they performed, the teachers would not be on stage with them.

The dress rehearsal added more people to the team. "Everyone works hard for the performance," said Jasper. "Our teachers make up the dances and teach us the steps. The musicians play the music. Someone else helps with the lights. The stage manager tells everyone where and when to do their jobs. Then we do the dancing."

"The parents help out, too, by coming to watch us. For sure, my family will be there!"

STRATEGY SKILL

Summarize
Summarize what happened during the dress rehearsal.

Performance Day

At last, the day of the performance arrived. Backstage, the dancers got ready. Then the audience took their seats.

Lights! Music! The show started! The sound of tapping feet filled the air.

The tap dancers crossed the stage together. Their feet were flying!

Ballet was next. The dancers glided across the floor with arms open. They looked as if they were dancing on air. The dance was long, but no one forgot the steps. All of their hard work had paid off.

Then the capoeira began. The dancers kicked and jumped. They clapped and sang in the roda.

When the dance was over, the dancers took a bow. The audience cheered. What a great performance!

The show was over, but the excitement did not end. Backstage, the dancers were happy. They had done a great job.

Their families gave them hugs. Their teachers were very **proud**.

"It was fun!" said Whitney.

"We did it!" said Jasper.

"We all did it together!"

Behind the Curtain with Sharon Dennis Wyeth

Sharon Dennis Wyeth knew she wanted to be a children's book writer when she was very young. Sharon says, "When I was a child, my favorite thing was reading. The library was my home away from home! Picking out a book all by myself made me feel powerful."

Sharon learned about performing when she was in high school. She sang in the chorus and acted in the school play.

 Find out more about Sharon Dennis Wyeth at **www.macmillanmh.com**

Other books written by Sharon Dennis Wyeth

 **Author's Purpose**

Sharon Dennis Wyeth wanted readers to learn about what it's like to perform. Have you ever been in a musical performance or a school play? What did you do? How did you feel? Write about it.

402

Comprehension Check

Retell the Story

Use the Retelling Cards to retell the selection.

Retelling Cards

Think and Compare

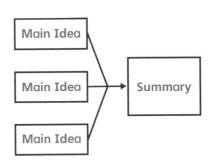

1. What did you learn about the young Alvin Ailey dancers? **Visualize: Summarize**

2. Reread pages 390–391. Why did Vic tell his tap dancing **students** that they had more work to do? Use the text to explain. **Analyze**

3. Would you enjoy being a student at the Alvin Ailey School? Why or why not? **Evaluate**

4. Why do you think dancers go to places like the Alvin Ailey School? **Apply**

5. How are the performers in "A Little Symphony" on pages 382–383 and *Dancing As a Team* alike? How are they different? **Reading/Writing Across Texts**

You'll Sing a Song and I'll Sing a Song

by Ella Jenkins

You'll sing a song
And I'll sing a song,
Then we'll sing a song together.
You'll sing a song
And I'll sing a song
In warm or wintery weather.

You'll play a tune
And I'll play a tune,
Then we'll play a tune together.
You'll play a tune
And I'll play a tune
In warm or wintery weather.

You'll hum a line
And I'll hum a line,
Then we'll hum a line together.
You'll hum a line
And I'll hum a line
In warm or wintery weather.

Connect and Compare

1. What are two groups of words in these lyrics that show alliteration? **Alliteration**

2. Reread pages 390–391 in *The Alvin Ailey Kids: Dancing As a Team*. How are the dance classes like the message in these lyrics? Explain why you think this. **Reading/Writing Across Texts**

 LOG ON Find out more about performing at **www.macmillanmh.com**

Write an Ad

My ad has precise details that tell people what they need to know.

I used the correct form of the verb have.

Come See The Best Play Ever!

You are invited to *see* the fourth graders perform a play based on The Wonderful Wizard of Oz, written by L. Frank Baum.

Don't miss Dorothy, the Tin Man, the Cowardly Lion, and the Scarecrow singing and dancing their way through Oz!

The show will be in the school auditorium on June 10 at 7:00 p.m. You'll have a great time!

Your Turn

Write an ad that will make people want to do something. The ad could make people want to buy a book, meet an author, or something else. Use precise words to make the meaning clear. Then use the Writer's Checklist to check your writing.

Writer's Checklist

☑ **Ideas:** Is my message clear? Do I use precise words that tell people what they need to know?

✓ **Voice:** Does my ad sound exciting? Does it make people want to do something?

✓ **Conventions:** Did I use the verb *have* correctly?

✓ **Word Choice:** Did I use strong verbs and other lively words to make my ad exciting?

407

On THE Farm

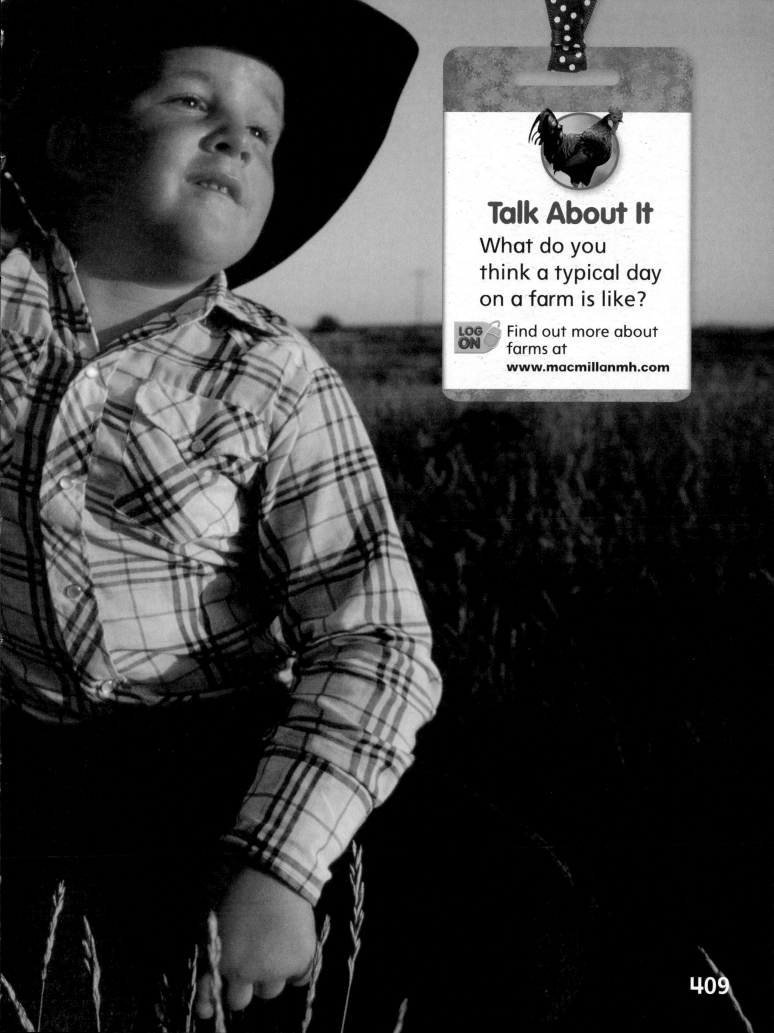

Talk About It

What do you think a typical day on a farm is like?

LOG ON Find out more about farms at
www.macmillanmh.com

IGGY PIG SAVES THE DAY

by Kevin Tormino

It was feeding time in the barnyard. Farmer Deb fed the pigs. But then, *BRRING*! The phone rang. Deb ran inside the house to get it. The animals waited and waited. They were getting **impatient**. What was taking Deb so long to return?

"BAA, BAA," said the very angry sheep. "MOO! MOO! MOO!" said the **furious** cows, stomping their feet. They were all mad and very hungry.

Iggy Pig decided to find Farmer Deb. He ran to her house to **snoop** around. First, he looked through the window. Then he looked in the kitchen. Where *was* Farmer Deb? What would make Farmer Deb come outside? Iggy wondered. Then he had an idea.

"HELP! HELP!" Iggy yelled. "Come right away."

Farmer Deb looked out the front door. She wondered what the **emergency** cry was for. What could be the problem?

"MOO! BAA!" the animals shouted together. "We **demand** that you feed us. That's an order!"

Deb dropped the phone and ran outside. She knew the animals wouldn't wait another minute.

Soon the animals were munching happily. Later, the cows sang to Iggy. "We **sincerely** thank you. We really mean it! MOO!"

Reread for **Comprehension**

Visualize
Cause and Effect
Visualizing, or forming pictures in your mind, can help you understand the cause and effect of events in a story. A cause is why something happens. An effect is what happens. Use the chart as you reread the story.

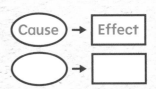

Comprehension

Genre
Fantasy is a story that has made-up characters, settings, or other things that could not happen in real life.

Visualize
Cause and Effect
As you read, use your Cause and Effect Chart.

Cause → Effect

Read to Find Out
How do the cows get Farmer Brown to do what they want?

Click, Clack, Moo
Cows That Type

by Doreen Cronin

illustrated by Betsy Lewin

Farmer Brown has a problem.
His cows like to type.
All day long he hears

Click, clack, **moo**.
Click, clack, **moo**.
Clickety, clack, **moo**.

At first, he couldn't believe his ears.
Cows that type?
Impossible!

Click, clack, **moo**.
Click, clack, **moo**.
Clickety, clack, **moo**.

Then, he couldn't believe his eyes.

Dear Farmer Brown,
The barn is very cold at night.
We'd like some electric blankets.

Sincerely,
The Cows

It was bad enough the cows had found the old typewriter in the barn, now they wanted electric blankets! "No way," said Farmer Brown. "No electric blankets."

So the cows went on strike. They left a note on the barn door.

Sorry.

We're closed.

No milk today.

Cause and Effect
What causes the cows to stop giving milk?

"No milk today!" cried Farmer Brown. In the background, he heard the cows busy at work:

Click, clack, **moo**.
Click, clack, **moo**.
Clickety, clack, **moo**.

420

The next day, he got
another note:

Dear Farmer Brown,
The hens are cold too.
They'd like electric
blankets.

Sincerely,
The Cows

The cows were growing **impatient** with the farmer. They left a new note on the barn door.

"No eggs!" cried Farmer Brown.
In the background he heard them.

Click, clack, **moo**.
Click, clack, **moo**.
Clickety, clack, **moo**.

"Cows that type. Hens on strike! Whoever heard of such a thing? How can I run a farm with no milk and no eggs!" Farmer Brown was **furious**.

Cause and Effect
Why is Farmer Brown so upset? What do you think he will do about the problem?

Farmer Brown got out his own typewriter.

Dear Cows and Hens:
There will be no electric blankets.
You are cows and hens.
I **demand** milk and eggs.

Sincerely,
Farmer Brown

Duck was a neutral party, so he brought the ultimatum to the cows.

428

The cows held an emergency meeting. All the animals gathered around the barn to snoop, but none of them could understand Moo.

All night long, Farmer Brown waited for an answer.

Duck knocked on the door early the next morning. He handed Farmer Brown a note:

Dear Farmer Brown,
We will exchange our typewriter
for electric blankets.
Leave them outside the barn door
and we will send Duck over
with the typewriter.

Sincerely,
The Cows

Farmer Brown decided this was
a good deal.

He left the blankets next to the barn
door and waited for Duck to come with
the typewriter.

The next morning he got a note:

Dear Farmer Brown,
The pond is quite boring.
We'd like a diving board.

Sincerely,
The Ducks

Click, clack, **quack**.
Click, clack, **quack**.
Clickety, clack, **quack**.

435

Farm Friends: Doreen and Betsy

Author **Doreen Cronin** and illustrator **Betsy Lewin** met for the first time after *Click, Clack, Moo* was published.

"I had a very, very loose picture in my head of what the animals might look like," Doreen says. "It was the publisher who decided that Betsy would be the illustrator for the book."

Betsy says that she and Doreen have become good friends and enjoy working together. "Each of us is eager for the other's comments and advice."

Other books written by Doreen Cronin and illustrated by Betsy Lewin

LOG ON Find out more about Doreen Cronin and Betsy Lewin at **www.macmillanmh.com**

Author's Purpose

Doreen Cronin wrote a funny story about farm animals. They give something up to get what they want. Did you ever give something up to get something else? Write about it.

Comprehension Check

Retell the Story

Use the Retelling Cards to retell the story.

Retelling Cards

Think and Compare

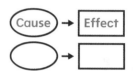

1. Why does Farmer Brown finally give the cows and hens the blankets? **Visualize: Cause and Effect**

2. Reread page 417. Why do the cows start writing notes to Farmer Brown? **Analyze**

3. Have you ever felt **impatient** like Farmer Brown? What advice would you give him? **Synthesize**

4. Why do you think real people might go on strike? **Synthesize**

5. How is the emergency in "Iggy Pig Saves the Day," on pages 410–411, like the one in *Click, Clack, Moo*? **Reading/Writing Across Texts**

Farming Corn

Farmers in Iowa usually grow the most corn in all of the United States. From April to November they work hard to grow as much corn as they can. Because corn grows best at certain times of the year, corn farmers follow a **schedule**. This tells them when to plant and when to pick, or **harvest**, the corn.

Spring is here. The corn farmers' work has just begun. Their first job is to plow the fields.

Plowing breaks up the soil and turns it over. Plowing makes the ground ready for the seeds to be planted. On big farms, farmers use planting machines to spread the corn seeds in the field.

───── July ─────						
Sunday	Monday	Tuesday	Wednesday	Thursday	Friday	Saturday
1	2	3	4	5	6	7
8	9	10	11	12	13	14
15	16	17	18	19	20	21
22	23	24	25	26	27	28
29	30	31				

───── August ─────						
Sunday	Monday	Tuesday	Wednesday	Thursday	Friday	Saturday
			1	2	3	4
5	6	7	8	9	10	11
12	13	14	15	16	17	18
19	20	21	22	23	24	25
26	27	28	29	30	31	

These calendars show two months that farmers work in the corn fields.

In July and August the farmers water the fields.

After several weeks, the plants begin to grow. Then it is time to weed the fields. The farmers use machines to make the soil loose around the growing plants. This helps kill the weeds. Rain and sun help the corn grow, too. The corn should be about two feet high by the Fourth of July.

Fall is an important season for the corn farmers. By then the corn should be 7 or 8 feet high. It is harvest time. Farmers pick the fully grown corn using a machine called a combine. After the **crop** is picked, farmers dry the corn so that it will last longer. When the farmers sell the corn, it is shipped to other states in train cars. This type of corn is called seed corn. It is used to feed farm animals all over the world.

Connect and Compare

1. According to the calendar, how many weeks do farmers water the fields? **Calendar**

2. Think about this article and *Click, Clack, Moo*. What other things might Farmer Brown have to do besides take care of the cows? **Reading/Writing Across Texts**

 Social Studies Activity

Research your favorite fruit or vegetable. Make a calendar that shows when it is planted and harvested.

LOG ON   Find out more about farming at **www.macmillanmh.com**

441

Writer's Craft

Precise Words
Good writers use **precise words** to show how they feel.

Precise words tell exactly how I feel.

I used <u>and</u> to combine sentences with the same subject.

12 Elm Street
Raleigh, NC 34567
May 16, 20--

Dear Editor,

   Why is the mayor increasing the speed limit on Main Street? I don't think this is safe for our town.

   Speeding cars are dangerous and could hurt wild animals and pets. If a car is going too fast, it won't be able to stop in time to let an animal finish crossing the street. I think the speed limit should stay low so animals in our town aren't put in danger.

                    Anthony P.

Your Turn

Write a letter to the editor of your town or school newspaper. Tell how you think or feel about something in your school or town. Choose precise words so that the reader will understand exactly how you feel and why. Use the Writer's Checklist to check your writing.

Writer's Checklist

☑ **Word Choice:** Did I use precise words that tell exactly how I feel and why?

✓ **Ideas:** Did I add details that make my reasons stronger?

✓ **Conventions:** Did I combine sentences with the same subject by using *and*?

✓ **Organization:** Is my letter easy to follow? Is my message clear?

Test Strategy

Right There
The answer is right there on the page. Skim for clues to find the answer.

MAKE A PIÑATA

BY ALLISON AGRESTI

Have you ever seen a piñata? A piñata is a container filled with treats. You can make a piñata. Then have your own piñata party!

You will need:
- a large balloon
- 2 feet of string
- strips of newspaper, 1 inch wide
- flour glue
- scissors
- tape
- wrapped treats
- colored tissue paper
- glue

Go on ▶

FOLLOW THESE STEPS:

Step 1. Make the piñata shape. Blow up a balloon and knot it. Tie a string around the knot. Then hang the balloon by the string.

Step 2. Make the piñata shell. Dip newspaper strips into the flour glue. Spread the strips onto the balloon one at a time. Overlap them so the balloon is covered completely. Let the strips dry. Then repeat this step. The balloon should have three layers in all.

Step 3. Add treats to the piñata. Make a three-inch-wide hole at the top of the piñata. Pop the balloon. Take it out. Fill the piñata with treats. Then tape the hole closed.

SAFETY RULES: Have an adult cut the hole in the piñata. Add treats that are small and light so no one gets hurt.

Go on ▶ 445

Step 4. Decorate the piñata. Use colorful tissue paper. Cut the paper into strips and interesting shapes. Glue or tape the tissue paper onto the piñata. Cover up all the newspaper.

Step 5. Have a piñata party. Hang your piñata from the ceiling of an open space. Get a long stick and a blindfold. With the blindfold on, try to break the piñata with the stick. Take turns with your friends. When it breaks, get the treats!

SAFETY RULES: Make sure an adult is present at the party. Give the person swinging the stick lots of room.

Tip

Skim for clues.

Directions:
Answer the questions.

1. **Why do you need a stick at a piñata party?**

   A to give the piñata its shape

   B to break the piñata

   C so the piñata looks pretty

   D so you can fill the piñata with treats

2. **How do you use the flour glue?**

   A to keep treats inside the piñata

   B to hold the stick safely

   C to layer newspaper strips on the balloon

   D to fix the piñata when it breaks

3. **What are two important safety rules when making and using a piñata?**

Writing Prompt

Write a letter to a family member. Explain why you think a piñata party would be fun to have and how you will help.

STOP 447

Glossary
What is a Glossary?

A glossary can help you find the **meanings** of words. If you see a word that you don't know, try to find it in the glossary. The words are in **alphabetical order**. **Guide words** at the top of each page tell you the first and last words on the page.

A **definition** is given for each word. An **example** shows the word used in a sentence. Each word is divided into **syllables**. Finally, the **part of speech** is given.

Guide Words

First word on the page   Last word on the page

Sample Entry

Definition

Main entry —— **exercise** To take part in an activity to keep your body healthy. *We **exercise** at the gym four days a week.*

Example sentence ——

Syllable division —— **ex•er•cise** *verb.* ———————— Part of Speech

449

Aa

accident A sad event that is not expected and in which people may be hurt. *Sarah hurt her knee when she had the bike accident.*
ac·ci·dent *noun.*

active Moving around or doing something much of the time. *Grandpa is still very active.*
ac·tive *adjective.*

ancient Having to do with times very long ago. *Scientists found an ancient city buried under layers of dirt.*
an·cient *adjective.*

attached Fastened. *Pedro attached this poster to the wall with tape.*
at·tached *verb.* Past tense of **attach.**

attention The act of watching or listening carefully. *The clown held the children's attention with his balloon shapes.*
at·ten·tion *noun.*

Bb

breathe To draw air into the lungs and then release it. *It can be hard to breathe after running a long race.*
breathe *verb.*

broken Damaged or in pieces. *We had to throw out the **broken** plate.*
bro·ken *adjective.*

buddy A close friend. *His **buddy** goes camping with him.*
bud·dy *noun.*

burst To break open suddenly. *The bag **burst** because I put too much in it.*
burst *verb.*

Cc

calm Not excited nor nervous. *Because we stayed **calm** during the fire, we got out safely.*
calm *adjective.*

carefully With care. *After checking the paragraph **carefully**, I found two mistakes.*
care·ful·ly *adverb.*

celebrate To show that something is important in a special way. *Americans **celebrate** the Fourth of July by marching in parades.*
cel·e·brate *verb.*

451

coach   A person who trains people who play sports. *My soccer **coach** made me practice a lot before the big game.*
coach *noun.*

company   A friend or friends. *I like to be surrounded by company.*
com·pa·ny *noun.*

confirm   To show to be true or correct. *Tomorrow's newspaper will **confirm** the report of a fire downtown.*
con·firm *verb.*

countries   Areas of land and the people who live there. *The **countries** of Canada and the United States are part of North America.*
coun·tries *plural noun.* Plural of **country**.

crop   A plant grown and gathered to be used for food or sold to earn money. *We have a huge **crop** of lettuce this year.*
crop *noun.*

452

cuddle To hold close in one's arms. *I like to **cuddle** my pet rabbit.*
cud·dle *verb.*

cultures The arts, beliefs, and customs that make up a way of life for a group of people. *I am studying the **cultures** of China and India.*
cul·tures *plural noun.* Plural of **culture**.

Dd

deaf Not able to hear, or not able to hear well. *Ralph uses sign language to speak to his mother because she is **deaf**.*
deaf *adjective.*

delicious Pleasing or delightful to taste or smell. *The apple pie cooking for dessert smelled **delicious**.*
de·li·cious *adjective.*

delighted Very pleased. *The child was **delighted** when she saw her presents.*
de·ligh·ted *adjective.*

demand To ask for with force. *The customer will **demand** his money back for the broken television.*
de·mand *verb.*

desert   A hot, dry, sandy area of land with few or no plants growing on it. *Plants that need a lot of water will not grow in a **desert**.*

des·ert *noun.*

different   Not the same as something else. *The teammates all had **different** numbers on their uniforms.*

dif·fer·ent *adjective.*

drifts   Moves because of a current of air or water. *When I stop rowing, my canoe **drifts** along the river.*

drifts *verb.* Present tense of **drift**.

drowns   To die by staying underwater and not being able to breathe. *A lifeguard watches the pool carefully to make sure that no one **drowns**.*

drowns *verb.* Present tense of **drown**.

Ee

effort   Hard work. *Climbing the five flights of stairs took much **effort**.*

ef·fort *noun.*

emergency   Having to do with something important or dangerous that needs fast action. *Use the **emergency** exit at the back of the theater in case of fire.*

e·mer·gen·cy *adjective.*

enjoyed Got joy or pleasure from; was happy with. *My family enjoyed last year's ski trip.*
en·joyed *verb.* Past tense of **enjoy**.

enormous Much greater than the usual size; very large. *Some dinosaurs were enormous compared with animals today.*
e·nor·mous *adjective.*

examines Looks at closely and carefully. *The coach always examines the hockey sticks to make sure they are not broken.*
ex·am·ines *verb.* Present tense of **examine**.

excited Made very happy about something. *The goalie's great play excited the fans.*
ex·cit·ed *verb.* Past tense of **excite**.

exercise To do an activity to help keep your body healthy. *We exercise at the gym four days a week.*
ex·er·cise *verb.*

Ff

favorite   A person or thing liked best. *Action movies are my* **favorite**.
fa·vor·ite *noun.*

festivals   Special activities or shows. *Our school hosts storytelling and film* **festivals** *every year.*
fes·ti·vals *plural noun.* Plural of **festival**.

flames   The glowing parts of a fire. *The campfire had big* **flames**.
flames *plural noun.* Plural of **flame**.

fluttered   Moved or flew with quick, light, flapping movements. *Moths* **fluttered** *around the light.*
flut·tered *verb.* Past tense of **flutter**.

forest   A large area of land covered with trees and other plants. *We camp out every year in the* **forest**.
for·est *noun.*

frantically   Done in a way that is wildly excited by worry or fear. *Maria searched **frantically** to find her lost keys.*
fran·tic·al·ly *adverb.*

friendship   The special feeling between friends. *I have always cherished her **friendship**.*
friend·ship *noun.*

furious   Very angry. *When I forgot to do my chores, Mom was **furious** with me.*
fu·ri·ous *adjective.*

Gg

gasped   Said while breathing in suddenly or with effort. *"Help!" **gasped** the struggling child.*
gasped *verb.* Past tense of **gasp**.

gently   Done carefully not to hurt someone or something. *Christopher **gently** stroked the kitten.*
gen·tly *adverb.*

giggled   Laughed in a silly or nervous way. *I **giggled** at my mom's funny joke.*
gig·gled *verb.* Past tense of **giggle**.

groan   To make a sad sound when you are unhappy, annoyed, or in pain. *I **groan** every time my coach makes me do push-ups.*
groan *verb.*

Hh

harvest   To pick and gather a crop. *The farmers will **harvest** the wheat in the fall.*
har·vest *verb.*

hatches   Comes from an egg. *The baby bird **hatches** from its egg when it is ready.*
hatches *verb.* Present tense of **hatch.**

hazards   Things that can cause harm or injury. *Ice, snow, rain, and fog are **hazards** to drivers.*
haz·ards *plural noun.* Plural of **hazard.**

heal   To become well or healthy again. *My cut will **heal** after I put a bandage on it.*
heal *verb.*

healthful   Good for people's health. *Walking is **healthful** for people.*
health·ful *adjective.*

heat   Great warmth or high temperature. *The **heat** from the fire kept the campers warm.*
heat *noun.*

hopeful Wanting or believing that something wished for will happen. *We are **hopeful** that the rain will stop before the field hockey game starts.*
hope·ful *adjective.*

hunger Pain or weakness caused by not eating enough food. *Some wild animals die from **hunger**.*
hun·ger *noun.*

Ii

imaginary Having a picture in the mind. *My brother made up an **imaginary** story.*
i·mag·i·nar·y *adjective.*

immigrant A person who comes to live in a country in which he or she was not born. *My grandmother was an **immigrant** to the United States from Haiti.*
im·mi·grant *noun.*

impatient Not able to put up with a delay or a problem calmly and without anger. *The editor became **impatient** when the book wasn't finished.*
im·pa·tient *adjective.*

informs Gives information to. *The firefighter **informs** the class about fire safety.*
in·forms *verb.* Present tense of **inform**.

Ll

language A way of telling ideas and feelings to others. *In Spain, the language used is Spanish.*
lan·guage *noun.*

librarian A person who is in charge of or works in a library. *The librarian helped me find a book about sharks.*
li·brar·i·an *noun.*

Mm

mammal A kind of animal that is warm-blooded and has a back bone. Female **mammals** make milk to feed their young. Most **mammals** are covered with fur or have some hair. *My teacher told me that a whale is a mammal, but a fish is not.*
mam·mal *noun.*

minerals Something found in nature that is not an animal or a plant. Salt, coal, and gold are **minerals**. *Some minerals, such as gold, are valuable.*
min·er·als *plural noun.* Plural of **mineral**.

mood The way that a person feels at a certain time. *I was in a good **mood** because I learned to ride a bike.*
mood *noun.*

Nn

neighbor A person, place, or thing that is near another. *A new **neighbor** moved in next door.*
neigh·bor *noun.*

normal Having or showing average health and growth. *The doctor said that it is **normal** for a baby to cry.*
nor·mal *adjective.*

nurse A person who takes care of sick people and teaches people how to stay healthy. *If you don't feel well at school, go to see the **nurse**.*
nurse *noun.*

Oo

obeys Does what one is told to do. *The dog **obeys** me when I tell him to stop running.*
o·beys *verb.* Present tense of **obey**.

orally Not written; using speech. *The story of my grandfather coming to America has been passed down **orally** in my family.* **o·ral·ly** *adverb.*

Pp

patient Being able to put up with problems or delays without getting angry or upset. *The people in line were **patient** even though they had waited an hour.* **pa·tient** *adjective.*

patterns The way that colors, shapes, or lines are placed. *I had several **patterns** to choose from: checks, dots, and stripes.* **pat·terns** *plural noun.* Plural of **pattern**.

peered Looked at closely to try to see something clearly. *The scientist **peered** through the telescope to study the stars.* **peered** *verb.* Past tense of **peer**.

perform To sing, act, or do something in public that takes skill. *The marching band will **perform** at the half-time show.* **per·form** *verb.*

personal Having to do with a person. *Denise kept her voice low so no one could hear her **personal** information when she was on the phone.* **per·son·al** *adjective.*

practiced   Doing something again and again until you do it well. *To learn the flute, I* **practiced** *every day.*

prac·ticed *verb.* Past tense of **practice.**

practices   When an activity is repeated in order to get better at doing it. *My swim team* **practices** *are three times a week.*

prac·tic·es *plural noun.* Plural of **practice.**

principal   The leader of the school. *The* **principal** *spoke at the assembly.*

prin·ci·pal *noun.*

promises   Statements that say something will or will not be done. *I made three* **promises** *to my mom today about doing my homework.*

prom·ises *plural noun.* Plural of **promise.**

proud   Having a good feeling about something that you or someone else did. *I am* **proud** *of the painting I made.*

proud *adjective.*

Rr

recognized   Knew and remembered from before. *I recognized my teacher in line when I went to the movies.* **rec·og·nized** *verb.* Past tense of **recognize**.

relatives   People who are part of a family. *My aunts, uncles, and cousins are some of my relatives.* **rel·a·tives** *plural noun.* Plural of **relative**.

remember   To think of something again; to not forget. *I haven't ridden a bike for ten years, but I remember how.* **re·mem·ber** *verb.*

rescued   Saved or freed. *The firefighter rescued the cat from the tree where it was stuck.* **res·cued** *verb.* Past tense of **rescue**.

route   A road or other course used for traveling. *We took a different route to the beach because of the traffic.* **route** *noun.*

Ss

safe   To be kept from danger. *We looked for a **safe** place to stay when the storm hit.*

safe *adjective.*

schedule   A list of times, events, or things to do. *I always check the train **schedule** before I leave for the train station.*

sched·ule *noun.*

seed   The part of a plant from which a new plant will grow. *We planted a pumpkin **seed** in the garden to try to grow pumpkins next year.*

seed *noun.*

serious   Dangerous. *The doctor told us that cancer is a **serious** illness.*

se·ri·ous *adjective.*

465

settled   To make a home in a place. *We **settled** in a large city when we moved to this country.*
set·tled *verb.* Past tense of **settle**.

share   To give some of what one person has to someone else. *Edgar will **share** his brownie with me.*
share *verb.*

signing   Showing words and letters with your hands and fingers. *Some people use **signing** to speak to one another.*
sign·ing *noun.*

sincerely   Done in an honest and true way. *I would like to thank you **sincerely** for your help.*
sin·cere·ly *adverb.*

snoop   To sneak around in order to find information. *I will **snoop** around my brother's room to see if he has candy.*
snoop *verb.*

snuggled   Lay close together or held closely for warmth or protection, or to show love. *I **snuggled** up against my mom during the thunderstorm.*
snug·gled *verb.* Past tense of **snuggle**.

stages   The different steps or times in a process. *During all **stages** of growth, a flower needs water.*
stag·es *plural noun.* Plural of **stage**.

starting Taking part in a game or contest at the beginning. *The **starting** lineup includes the strongest players on the team.* **star·ting** *adjective.*

students People who go to a school. *The fifth grade has one hundred **students** this year.* **stu·dents** *plural noun.* Plural of **student.**

sunlight The light of the sun. *We enjoyed the bright **sunlight** at the beach.* **sun·light** *noun.*

swung Moved back and forth. *We **swung** back and forth on the monkey bars.* **swung** *verb.* Past tense of **swing.**

Tt

tell To give information. *The firefighters **tell** us how to stay safe.* **tell** *verb.*

thinning Becoming thin; decreasing in number. *Grandpa's hair is **thinning.*** **thin·ning** *adjective.*

tips Some helpful information. *My teacher gave me some **tips** for how to spell better.* **tips** *plural noun.* Plural of **tip.**

tomorrow The day after today. *If today is Monday, then **tomorrow** is Tuesday.* **to·mor·row** *noun.*

tradition A custom or belief that is passed down from parents to children. *It is my family's* **tradition** *to eat blueberry pie on Thanksgiving.*
tra·di·tion *noun.*

trust To believe that someone or something is true or honest. *I* **trust** *my mom to tell me the truth.*
trust *verb.*

tryouts Showing one's skill or ability to join a team or group. *I went to soccer* **tryouts,** *hoping to earn a place on the team.*
try·outs *plural noun.* Plural of **tryout.**

Uu

unable Not having the power or skill to do something; not able. *I was* **unable** *to reach the light switch because it is too high.*
un·a·ble *adjective.*

uniform The special or official clothes that the members of a group wear. Soldiers, police officers, and some students wear **uniforms**. *My baseball* **uniform** *is green and yellow.*
u·ni·form *noun.*

Vv

valid   Correct based on facts or proof. *My experiment proved that my theory was **valid**.*
val·id *adjective.*

vanished   Gone from sight. *The moon **vanished** behind the clouds.*
van·ished *verb.* Past tense of **vanish**.

Ww

whisper   To speak in a very quiet voice. *I will **whisper** a secret to my friend.*
whis·per *verb.*

wonderful   Very good. *My uncle cooked a **wonderful** dinner that my family enjoyed.*
won·der·ful *adjective.*

wrinkled   Made a fold, ridge, or line in a smooth surface. *I **wrinkled** my shirt so much that my dad had to iron it.*
wrin·kled *verb.* Past tense of **wrinkle**.

Yy

young   Not old. *A "joey" is what we call a **young** kangaroo.*
young *adjective.*

469

Acknowledgments

The publisher gratefully acknowledges permission to reprint the following copyrighted materials:

Book Cover, ARROWHAWK by Lola M. Schaefer, illustrated by Gabi Swiatkowska. Text copyright © 2004 by Lola M. Schaefer. Illustrations copyright © 2004 by Gabi Swiatkowska. Reprinted by permission of Henry Holt and Company, LLC.

Book Cover, A BIRTHDAY BASKET FOR TÍA by Pat Mora, illustrated by Cecily Lang. Text copyright © 1992 by Pat Mora. Illustrations copyright © 1992 by Cecily Lang. Reprinted by permission of Aladdin Books, an imprint of Simon & Schuster Children's Publishing.

Book Cover, CECIL'S GARDEN by Holly Keller. Copyright © 2002 by Holly Keller. Reprinted by permission of Greenwillow Books, an imprint of HarperCollins Publishers.

Click, Clack, Moo: Cows That Type by Doreen Cronin, illustrated by Betsy Lewin. Text copyright © 2000 by Doreen Cronin. Illustrations copyright © 2000 by Betsy Lewin. Reprinted with permission from Simon & Schuster Books for Young Readers, an imprint of Simon & Schuster Children's Publishing Division.

Book Cover, DADDY CALLS ME MAN by Angela Johnson, illustrated by Rhonda Mitchell. Text copyright © 1997 by Angela Johnson. Illustrations copyright © 1997 Rhonda Mitchell. Reprinted by permission of Orchard Books.

Book Cover, THE DAY THE BABIES CRAWLED AWAY by Peggy Rathmann. Copyright © 2003 by Peggy Rathmann. Reprinted by permission of Penguin Group (USA), Inc.

Book Cover, DUCK FOR PRESIDENT by Doreen Cronin, illustrated by Betsy Lewin. Text copyright © 2004 by Doreen Cronin. Illustrations copyright © 2004 by Betsy Lewin. Reprinted by permission of Simon & Schuster Books for Young Readers, an imprint of Simon & Schuster Children's Publishing Division.

Farfallina and Marcel by Holly Keller. Copyright © 2002 by Holly Keller. Reprinted with permission from Greenwillow Books, an imprint of HarperCollins Publishers.

Book Cover, GIGGLE, GIGGLE, QUACK by Doreen Cronin, illustrated by Betsy Lewin. Text copyright © 2002 by Doreen Cronin. Illustrations copyright © 2002 by Betsy Lewin. Reprinted by permission of Simon & Schuster Books for Young Readers, an imprint of Simon & Schuster Children's Publishing Division.

Book Cover, A GIRAFFE CALF GROWS UP by Joan Hewett and Richard Hewett. Text copyright © 2004 by Joan Hewett. Photographs copyright © 2004 by Richard R. Hewett. Reprinted by permission of Carolrhoda Books, a division of Lerner Publishing Group.

Book Cover, GOOD NIGHT, GORILLA by Peggy Rathmann. Text and illustrations copyright © 1994 by Peggy Rathmann. Reprinted by permission of Penguin Group (USA), Inc.

Book Cover, THE GROUCHY LADYBUG by Eric Carle. Copyright © 1977, 1996 by Eric Carle. Reprinted by permission of HarperCollins Publishers.

A Harbor Seal Pup Grows Up by Joan Hewett and Richard Hewett Text copyright © 2002 by Joan Hewett. Photographs copyright © 2002 by Richard Hewett. Reprinted with permission from Carolrhoda Books, Inc., a division of Lerner Publishing Group.

Book Cover, HARVEST by George Ancona. Copyright © 2001 by George Ancona. Reprinted by permission of Marshall Cavendish Corporation.

Head, Body, Legs: A Story from Liberia by Won-Ldy Paye and Margaret H. Lippert, illustrated by Julie Paschkis. Text copyright © 2002 by Won-Ldy Paye and Margaret H. Lippert. Illustrations copyright © 2002 by Julie Paschkis. Reprinted with permission from Henry Holt and Company, LLC.

Book Cover, HENRY AND MUDGE AND THE SNEAKY CRACKERS by Cynthia Rylant, illustrated by Suçie Stevenson. Text copyright © 1998 by Cynthia Rylant. Illustrations copyright © 1998 by Suçie Stevenson. Reprinted by permission of Aladdin Books, an imprint of Simon & Schuster Children's Publishing Division.

Book Cover, JULIUS by Angela Johnson, illustrated by Dav Pilkey. Text copyright © 1993 by Angela Johnson. Illustrations copyright © 1993 by Dav Pilkey. Reprinted by permission of Orchard Books.

Book Cover, A KOALA JOEY GROWS UP by Joan Hewett and Richard Hewett. Text copyright © 2004 by Joan Hewett. Photographs copyright © 2004 by Richard R. Hewett. Reprinted by permission of Carolrhoda Books, a division of Lerner Publishing Group.

Book Cover, LET'S DANCE by George Ancona. Copyright © 1998 by George Ancona. Reprinted by permission of Morrow Junior Books, a division of William Morrow and Company, Inc.

Book Cover, THE MIXED-UP CHAMELEON by Eric Carle. Copyright © 1975, 1984 by Eric Carle. Reprinted by permission of HarperCollins Publishers.

Mr. Putter and Tabby Pour the Tea by Cynthia Rylant, illustrated by Arthur Howard. Text copyright © 1994 by Cynthia Rylant. Illustrations copyright © 1994 by Arthur Howard. Reprinted with permission from Harcourt, Inc.

Book Cover, MRS. CHICKEN AND THE HUNGRY CROCODILE by Won-Ldy Paye and Margaret H. Lippert, illustrated by Julie Paschkis. Text copyright © 2003 by Won-Ldy Paye and Margaret H. Lippert. Illustrations copyright © 2003 by Julie Paschkis. Reprinted by permission of Henry Holt and Company, LLC.

My Name Is Yoon by Helen Recorvits, illustrated by Gabi Swiatkowska. Text copyright © 2003 by Helen Recorvits. Illustrations copyright © 2003 by Gabi Swiatkowska. Reprinted with permission from Frances Foster Books, a division of Farrar, Straus and Giroux.

Officer Buckle and Gloria by Peggy Rathmann. Text and illustrations copyright © 1995 by Peggy Rathmann. Reprinted with permission from G.P. Putnam's Sons, a division of Penguin Putnam Books for Young Readers.

Book Cover, POPPLETON by Cynthia Rylant, illustrated by Mark Teague. Text copyright © 1997 by Cynthia Rylant. Illustrations copyright © 1997 by Mark Teague. Reprinted by permission of Scholastic Inc.

"The Puppy" from RING A RING O' ROSES: FINGER PLAYS FOR PRE-SCHOOL CHILDREN. Reprinted with permission from Flint Public Library.

Book Cover, THE RAINBOW TULIP by Pat Mora, illustrated by Elizabeth Sayles. Text copyright © 1999 by Pat Mora. Illustrations copyright © 1999 by Elizabeth Sayles. Reprinted by permission of Penguin Group (USA), Inc.

Book Cover, SOMETHING BEAUTIFUL by Sharon Dennis Wyeth, illustrated by Chris K. Soentpiet. Text copyright © 1998 by Sharon Dennis Wyeth. Illustrations copyright © 1998 by Chris K. Soentpiet. Reprinted by permission of Dragonfly Books, an imprint of Random House, Inc.

Book Cover, THAT'S MINE, HORACE by Holly Keller. Copyright © 2000 by Holly Keller. Reprinted by permission of Greenwillow Books, an imprint of HarperCollins Publishers.

The Tiny Seed by Eric Carle. Copyright © 1987 by Eric Carle Corp. Reprinted with permission from Aladdin Paperbacks, an imprint of Simon & Schuster Children's Publishing Division.

Book Cover, TOMBOY TROUBLE by Sharon Dennis Wyeth, illustrated by Lynne Woodcock Cravath. Text copyright © 1998 by Sharon Dennis Wyeth. Illustrations copyright © 1998 by Lynn Woodcock Cravath. Reprinted by permission of Random House Children's Books, a division of Random House, Inc.

"You'll Sing a Song and I'll Sing a Song" from THE ELLA JENKINS SONG BOOK FOR CHILDREN by Ella Jenkins. Text copyright © 1966 by Ella Jenkins. Reprinted with permission from Oak Publications (A Division of Embassy Music Corporation).

"You-Tú" from POCKET POEMS by Charlotte Pomerantz. Text copyright © 1960 by Charlotte Pomerantz. Reprinted with permission from Dutton Children's Books, a division of Penguin Young Readers Group.

ILLUSTRATION

Cover Illustration: Robert Giusti

14-31: Ed Martinez. 42-65: Arthur Howard. 68: Daniel Del Valle. 108-109: Marylin Hafner. 110: Rob Schuster. 114: Jason Wolff. 116-143: Gabi Swiatkowska. 148: Daniel Del Valle. 158-183: Eric Carle. 186: Daniel Del Valle. 212: (bc) Richard Hewitt. 214-215: Jo Parry. 216: Daniel Del Valle. 232-233: Marisol Sarrazin. 234-257: Holly Keller. 259-260: Andrea Tachiera. 262: Daniel Del Valle. 268-285: E.B. Lewis. 286-289: Rob Schuster. 298-299: Diane Greenseid. 300-327: Julie Paschkis. 330: Jim Kelly. 334-335: Diane Greenseid. 336-361: Peggy Rathmann. 364: Robert Schuster. 402: (cr) Lynne Woodcock Cravath. 406: Daniel Del Valle. 410-411: Kenneth Spengler. 412-437: Betsy Lewin. 444-446: Sally Vitsky. 448-449: Karen Dugan.

PHOTOGRAPHY

All photographs are by Macmillan McGraw-Hill (MMH) except as noted below

10-11: ©Charles Gupton/CORBIS. 11: Siede Preis/Getty Images, Inc. 12: (tr) Ariel Skelley/CORBIS; (bl) Royalty-free/CORBIS. 13: David Hanover/Stone/Getty Images, Inc. 30: (tr) Cheron Bayna; (cl) Deborah Chabrian. 32: (bl) Bob Daemmrich/The Image Works. 32-33: (bkgd) Taxi/Getty Images. 33: (cr) Stone/Getty Images, Inc.;(br) Royalty-Free/CORBIS. 34: (tr) Royalty-Free/CORBIS; (bl) Michael Newman/Photoedit Inc. 35: Bob Daemmrich/The Image Works. 36: Mike Powell/Getty Images, Inc. 37: Burke/Triolo/Brand X Pictures/ Getty Images, Inc. 38-39: (2) © Ariel Skelley/CORBIS. 39: (tr) David Buffington/Getty Images, Inc. 40: (t) Burke/Triolo Productions/ Brand X Pictures/Getty Images, Inc.; (bl) Tim Ridley/DK Images; (bc) Erwin Bud Nielsen/Index Stock Imagery. 41: Jim Cummins/ Taxi/Getty Images. 64: (tl) courtesy of Cynthia Rylant; (cr) Michael Papo. 66: Stone/Getty Images. 67: (c) Ellen B. Senisi/The Image Works; (bkgd) Photodisc. 68: Steve Cole/Getty Images, Inc. 69: Asia Images/Getty Images, Inc. 70-71: Lucy Nicholson/Reuters/Newscom. 72: Walter S. Mitchell III. 73: Courtesy USDA Forest Service. 74: AP-Wide World Photos. 75: Reuters/Lucy Nicholson/Newscom. 76: (tl) Justin Sullivan/Getty Images, Inc/Newscom; (bl) AP-Wide World Photos; (tr) Hans Gutknecht/LA Daily News/Polaris. 77: Fred Greaves/Reuters/Newscom. 80: Digital Vision. 81: (c) Dian Lofton for TFK; (cr) Dian Lofton for TFK; (br) C Squared Studios/Photodisc/ Getty Images, Inc.; (bl) Photodisc/Getty Images, Inc. 82-83: (bkgd) ©Martin Specht/Peter Arnold, Inc. 83: (tr) George Ancona. 84: (b) Richard T. Nowitz/ CORBIS. 84: (b) Richard T. Nowitz/Corbis; (tc) Digital vision/Getty Images, Inc.; (tr) Digital vision/Getty Images, Inc. 85: (cr) Myrleen Ferguson Cate/Photo Network/Alamy; (tr) Digital vision/Getty Images, Inc.; (br) Digital vision/Getty Images, Inc. 87-105: George Ancona. 107: George Ancona. 110: Dennis MacDonald/Photo Edit Inc. 112-113: (bkgd) ©Jim Cummins/CORBIS. 113: David Buffington/Getty Images, Inc. 142: courtesy of Farrar, Straus & Giroux. 144: (t) Dynamic Graphics/IT Stock Free/Alamy; (b) Brand X Pictures/PunchStock. 145: Jeff Greenberg/Alamy. 146: (bkgd) Tim Tadder/AP Images; (inset) Ken Cavanagh for MMH. 147: Jeff Greenberg/Alamy. 149: Dave King/Dorling Kindersley/Getty Images, Inc. 150: Royalty-Free/CORBIS. 151: Jonathan & Angela/ Taxi/Getty Images. 152: Jonathan & Angie Scott/ImageState/

PictureQuest. 154-155: (bkgd) Masterfile. 155: (tr) C Squared Studios/ Getty Images, Inc. 156: Gijsbert van Frankenhuyzen/Dembinsky Photo Associates. 157: Miriam Silverstein/Animals Animals/Earth Scenes. 182: John Dolan. 186: Laura Dwight/Photo Edit Inc. 187: C Squared Studios/Photodisc Green/Getty Images, Inc. 188-189: (bkgd) Fred Whitehead/Animals Animals/Earth Scenes. 189: (tr) Photodisc/Getty Images, Inc. 190: Tony Savino/The Image Works, Inc. 192-211: (bkgd) Richard Hewett. 212: (tl) courtesy of Joan Hewett. 212: (cr) courtesy of Richard Hewett. 213: (br) Richard Hewitt. 217: Larime Photo/Dembinsky Photo Associates. 218-219: Comstock Images. 220: (tr) Keith Brofsky/Photodisc/Getty Images, Inc.; (bcr) Suzanne Dunn/The Image Works. 221: Pete Saloutos/CORBIS. 222: Ryan McVay/Photodisc/Getty Images. 223: Adamsmith/ Taxi/Getty Images, Inc. 224: Adamsmith/Taxi/Getty Images, Inc. 225: Adamsmith/Taxi/Getty Images. 226: CORBIS. 228: Ryan McVay/Photodisc/Getty Images. 229: (bc) Dian Lofton for TFK. 229: (br) C Squared Studios/Photodisc/Getty Images, Inc.; (bl) Photodisc/Getty Images, Inc. 230-231: (bkgd) MARTIN HARVEY/ GALLO IMAGES/CORBIS. 231: (tr) Photodisc/Getty Images, Inc. 256: courtesy of Holly Keller. 258: Frank Greenway/DK Images. 259: NHPA/Stephen Dalton. 262: Michael Newman/Photo Edit Inc. 263: Patricia Doyle/Photographer's Choice/Getty Images, Inc. 264-265: (bkgd) TIMOTHY O'KEEFE/Index Stock Imagery. 265: (tr) Royalty Free/CORBIS. 266: Ariel Skelley/CORBIS. 267: Photodisc Green/ Getty Images, Inc. 284: (tl) courtesy of Simon and Schuster; (cl) courtesy of Eric Velasquez; (baseball) Photodisc. 286: Rubberball Productions/Getty Images, Inc. 287: Photodisc/Getty Images, Inc. 288: Tim Pannell/CORBIS. 289: Lawrence Migdale/Getty Images, Inc. 290: Megumi Takamura/Dex Image/Getty Images, Inc. 291: Mary Kate Denny/Photo Edit Inc. 292: Ariel Skelley/CORBIS. 293: Peter Sterling/Taxi/Getty Images, Inc. 294: Fredrik Skold/ Photographer's Choice/Getty Images, Inc. 296-297: (bkgd) Gabe Palmer/CORBIS. 297: (tr) Geostock/Getty Images, Inc. 326: (tr) courtesy of Won-Ldy Paye; (cl) courtesy of Julie Paschkis. 328: Stone/Getty Images, Inc. 330: Wetzel & Company. 331: ©CORBIS. 332-333: (bkgd) Paul Barton/CORBIS. 333: (tr) Dynamic Graphics Group/Creatas/Alamy. 360: courtesy of Peggy Rathmann. 362: Kathy McLaughlin/The Image Works, Inc. 363: (tr) Geri Engberg/The Image Works, Inc.; (bl) Richard Hutchings/Photo Edit Inc.; (bc) Richard Hutchings/Photo Edit Inc.; (br) Richard Hutchings/Photo Edit Inc. 364: Photodisc Green/Getty Images, Inc. 365: Michael Newman/Photo Edit Inc. 366: David Nagel/Allsport Concepts/Getty Images, Inc. 367: (c) Ablestock/Hemera Technologies/Alamy; (tr) Alaska Stock LLC/Alamy. 368-369: Maria Stenzel & Mark O. Thiessen/ National Geographic Image Collection. 370: Norbert Wu. 371: Marcos Brindicci/Reuters/Newscom. 372: Robert F. Walters. 373: (bl) Edward Degginger/Bruce Coleman Inc. 373: (br) Millard H. Sharp/ Photo Researchers, Inc. 374: Mike Hettwer/National Geographic Image Collection. 375: Will Burgess/Reuters/Newscom. 376: David Krause/Madagascar Ankizy Fund. 378: Ross Whitaker/The Image Bank/Getty Images. 379: (c) Dian Lofton for TFK; (bl) Photodisc/ Getty Images, Inc.; (br) C Squared Studios/Photodisc/Getty Images, Inc.; (cr) Dian Lofton for TFK. 380-381: (bkgd) Keren Su/CORBIS. 381: (tr) Photodisc/Getty Images, Inc. 382: (b) Paul Slocombe; (l) Comstock/Getty Images, Inc. 383: (t) Digital Vision Ltd./Getty Images, Inc.; (cr) Ingram Publishing/Alamy. 384-401: Beatriz Schiller. 402: courtesy of Sharon Dennis Wyeth. 403: Beatriz Schiller. 404: ©BananaStock / Alamy. 405: Photodisc Green/Getty Images, Inc. 406: Image 100/Royalty Free/CORBIS. 407: Ed Zurga/AP-Wide World Photos. 408-409: (bkgd) Annie Griffiths Belt/CORBIS. 409: (tr) F. Schussler/PhotoLink/Getty Images, Inc. 436: courtesy of Simon and Schuster. 438-439: (b) Colin Hiskins/Cordaiy Photo Library Ltd./CORBIS. 439: (c) Sylvain Saustier/CORBIS. 440: Bill Stormont/ CORBIS. 441: FoodPix/Getty Images. 442: MTPA Stock/Masterfile. 443: Rachel Epstein/Photo Edit Inc. 449: Ariel Skelley/CORBIS. 450: (t) Cindy Charles/Photo Edit Inc.; (b) Ronnie Kaufman/CORBIS. 451: (br) Ariel Skelley/Masterfile; (bl) Ryan McVay/Getty Images. 452: (l) Zoran Milich/Masterfile; (r) Nigel Cattlin/Photo Researchers, Inc. 453: (l) CORBIS. 454: (l) Bruce Heinemann/Getty Images.; (r) Steve Allen/Brand X Pictures/AGE Fotostock. 455: